INFERTILITY AND PTSD

THE UNCHARTED STORM

Joanna Flemons, LCSW, CPC

ISBN: 1542615542
ISBN 13: 9781542615549

The ideas and suggestions throughout this book are not meant to be used as a substitute for seeking advice, diagnosis and treatment from a trained mental health professional and / or physician. This author is not providing any professional or psychological services to the reader and will not be held liable for any sort of losses arising from any suggestions, data or material in this book.

Warrior -
That light is still in you.
Though it's changed, the flame is still blazing.

— ❤ —

TABLE OF CONTENTS

INTRODUCTION

"Hope is medicine for a soul that's sick and tired."
— Rev. Eric Jonas Swensson

The turbulent unpredictability and repetitive loss of infertility can shatter your dreams and change the way you view yourself and the world. Trauma upends the comforts and familiarity of your life before infertility, leaving you to question if it is even possible to return to the life and the person you were before trauma.

The truth is that many who face infertility challenges do ultimately recover and thrive again with renewed strength and stamina. However, not everyone will respond in the same way. Your capacity to cope, recover, and function both during and after infertility and trauma(s) can be impacted by many challenging factors.

- Everyday triggers of loss.
- Limited time to recover from one loss to the next.
- Inadequate support systems.
- Lack of insurance coverage for fertility treatments.
- Financial and other extraneous pressures.
- Prior trauma(s) and loss(es).
- Physical and psychological challenges.
- Lack of resources and opportunities.
- Social consequences.

Research now indicates that certain experiences occurring during infertility can also trigger symptoms of posttraumatic stress disorder (PTSD) in some. PTSD is a gripping trauma and stressor-related disorder triggered by exposure to a terrifying event of actual or threatened death, serious injury or sexual violation where a person feels completely helpless and unable to prevent what has happened.[1] The trauma event is so overwhelming that the brain is unable to fully process and catalog the memory as *finished* and *complete*. Without resolution, the brain and body continually relive and re-experience the trauma as though it were happening all over again. These intrusive symptoms can linger for months or even years and resurface at unpredictable times throughout life. Many struggling with PTSD will also experience a significant paradigm shift in their thinking as their quality of life dramatically changes.

- Will I ever feel the same as before?
- Why do I feel lost and disconnected from my life?
- Why am I losing control over my body?
- Why am I numb to my feelings?
- Why can't I sleep anymore?
- Why am I struggling to trust my own judgement?
- What is the point of this?
- Why don't I want to be around others anymore?
- Why can't I control my thoughts?
- Why can't I concentrate?
- Am I going crazy?
- Why am I so anxious all the time?
- Why can't I control my moods?

- Why do I dread the future?

- Is there something wrong with me?

- Who am I now?

Over the years, I have spent thousands of hours helping traumatized clients rebuild and reorient to life after terrifying and overwhelming events have shattered and foundationally disorganized many parts of their former realities. I have seen that infertility, ectopic pregnancy, recurrent pregnancy loss, stillbirth and other facets of this arduous journey can result in PTSD symptoms.

Facing infertility in the present while regulating intrusive PTSD symptoms from past trauma and loss is an enormous challenge. Many are left questioning their competency, stability and even sanity at times, as the physical and psychological toll is immense.

The following chapters provide answers to the questions that arise from complex trauma and PTSD. Throughout this book, I will highlight ideas, proven techniques and evidence-based treatment suggestions to consider. This book is not intended to be used as a substitute for seeking advice, diagnosis and/or treatment from a trained mental health specialist or physician. There is a list of trauma specialists and trauma resources located in the *Resources* section at the end of this book.

Be mindful that as you read this material, some of it may trigger current or unresolved trauma symptoms. Some of the condensed information may be uncomfortable to read and assimilate. Specifically, it may not be the right time to read the book. Or, it might be wise to read it slowly, putting it aside to take a break if it is too upsetting or overwhelming. Resume reading when you feel ready. Alternately, it might be better to explore some of the outlined suggestions and ideas listed at each chapter's conclusion to help reduce the effects of the trauma you have experienced. The choice is entirely yours.

Trauma steals your sense of personal authority and PTSD creates a profound loss of self. Re-establishing personal power and restoring the "self" after trauma is a process. Symptom relief takes time. It is common to feel worse before feeling better when working through trauma. Make sure that you are taking extra care of yourself during this time. Actively engage in satisfying activities such as walking your dog, going for a drive, spending time outdoors, listening to music, reading and/or any other activity you find enjoyable.

Some of the outlined scenarios in this book may be relevant to your situation, while others may not represent your unique journey. Remember each person's experience of infertility and/or PTSD may not be the same, just as the way a person copes and recovers from trauma tends to vary considerably from one person to another.

Although this book is written for those who are struggling with current or past infertility trauma and related PTSD, it is also a great resource for anyone simply wanting to learn more on the subject. Sometimes it's hard to know how to support and encourage loved ones who are going through an insurmountable personal crisis, especially if you haven't experienced the same journey. Your commitment to learning about what they are going through can go a long way.

I am indebted to the scientific community, field experts, voices of those who have experienced infertility or who are currently walking this journey, and to those who develop the advanced technologies for relevant education and research that empowers those who have been traumatized. In addition to sharing some of their work, I will also share insights gathered through my own observations and clinical work that I hope will bring significant validation to you.

Recovering from trauma and PTSD is a continuous process that begins with education. The people who have the greatest capacity for recovery are those who learn about their symptoms and are willing to implement a compassionate and customized plan of care for their individual recovery. Despite the trauma(s) in your life, you can ultimately thrive. There is hope.

Joanna Flemons, LCSW, CPC

CHAPTER 1:

INFERTILITY

In the blink of an eye, life changes.
— Unknown

Mary had dreamed of being a mother since she was a little girl. The longing was innate. Now, decades later, she reflected on the cruelty of wanting something so deeply, only to have it "ripped away" time and again.

Twelve weeks pregnant, Mary was finally considering sharing the news with her family. It had been a long hard road reaching this place again, but she was allowing herself to cautiously embrace hope one more time.

Mary ultimately disclosed the good news. But now, just weeks later, she faced the reality of yet another miscarriage. Her questions represent the common experience of shock and disbelief in the aftermath of trauma: "How is this possible?" - "Why is this happening to us again?" - "We are good people. What did we ever do to deserve this?"

Her spouse Brian could barely endure the pain of witnessing Mary's suffering anymore. He, too, was grief-stricken and often torn between the role of being strong for Mary while trying to also tend to his own emotional processes.

He desperately missed the old Mary – the wife who used to laugh, was full of life, and who enjoyed every part of their life together. Brian wondered if things would ever return to the way they were before.

Infertility continued to disrupt the security and predictability of their life together. It was never in the plan. The vision for their future was in constant flux. Traumatic grief and loss consumed years of their lives together, future planning, finances, family, friendships, and so much more. Life didn't feel the same anymore. The repetitive traumas were too much to bear. Infertility was devastating their lives.

"Infertility is defined as a 'disease of the reproductive system' and results in disability. It is a global public health issue."[1]

– World Health Organization (WHO)

Infertility is a consuming disease and personal crisis that strikes individuals each day. In populations under age 60, the World Health Organization ranks infertility in women the fifth highest serious global disability.[2] One-third of infertility is attributed to a male factor while another third is attributed to a female factor. The remaining third arises from either problems in both parties or from some unidentified issue.[3]

According to the Centers for Disease Control and Prevention's National Survey of Family Growth, 12 out of 100 women aged 15 to 44 have received infertility services.[4]

The diagnosis of infertility and the inability to conceive or sustain a pregnancy to full-term leaves individuals and couples reeling in the aftermath of loss. Infertility creates a psychological shock that can leave individuals disputing the diagnosis initially, and sometimes seeking a second opinion to confirm the distressing reality.[5]

A study of 200 couples who were seen continuously at a fertility clinic revealed that 50% of the women and 15% of the men described infertility as the most upsetting experience of their lives.[6] In this same study, men also reported having the same psychological experience of infertility as women, including low self-esteem and stigmatization when they learned the medical issue was theirs.[7]

In 1993, one study found that the psychological symptoms of infertility in women is equivalent to the psychological symptoms seen in women facing diagnoses of cancer, cardiac rehabilitation and hypertension.[8] Infertility is rarely anticipated, and any pre-existing beliefs about the feasibility of conception are painfully abolished.

Infertility remains a silent epidemic. Many people who suffer don't speak out about their struggles for an assortment of reasons, including feelings of shame and inadequacy. According to a survey administered in 2009, 61% of couples said they hide their infertility struggle from family and friends.[9]

*"I thought having a baby when I was 'ready' would be easy.
I was wrong. To this day it baffles my mind that nowhere,
in not one science class I took in 16 years of school,
did any teacher once mention this as a possibility
in my future life as a wannabe mother."* [10, 11]

– Monica Fike, Contributing Author
www.theguardian.com

The fertility journey varies considerably from person to person. From the timeline experienced, the approaches to pregnancy and treatments pursued, to the coping mechanisms and outcomes, no two stories are the same. You might attempt to become pregnant naturally using home remedies. Or, you might pursue fertility drugs and reproductive treatment. You might eventually choose to create your family through options such as adoption, fostering, and so on. Or, you might ultimately decide to stop trying altogether and remain involuntarily child-free.

While life seems to forge ahead effortlessly and steadily for so many, infertility can leave you feeling left behind, forgotten and unqualified to embrace the experience your heart longs for. Your emotional journey is highly personal. Sometimes it's hard to explain to others what you yourself cannot understand or correct.

Infertility hurts. It is a path no one chooses. It is a complete diversion from the original plan. Over time, it can leave you feeling uprooted from your core foundation, as the world you once knew becomes vastly changed and disturbingly unreliable.

"Infertility is like a spectator sport. I feel like I'm the only one in the bleachers watching everyone play, and I'm unqualified to join the team."[12]

– Meredith Hodge, Blogger
www.itspositiveliving.com

CHAPTER 2:

THE DELAY

"Trauma carves a painful dividing line in the survivor's personal narrative, a line that splices his life in two; there's the person he was before and the person he's become since. Profoundly undermined, he is lonely, fearful, disoriented, and unnerved by the certainty that he is not who he thought and indeed the world is no longer amenable to past interpretation."

– Belleruth Naparstek, ACSW, BCD
*Invisible Heroes: Survivors of
Trauma and How They Heal*

The haze is thick, and there's no end in sight. This uncharted territory isn't on any map, and valuable seasons of life have now passed. This painful timeline and delay has a powerful grip on your life. It is one you cannot shake.

Month after month, year after year, triggers and reminders of your loss can barge in daily unannounced. This pain can't be avoided, even with constant vigilance. You've tried your best to manage, but this chronic reproductive journey expands into every other part of your life.

There is also a distinguished change and shift in your identity. There's the "you before" infertility, and the "you now." This confusion only exacerbates your self-esteem and confidence, leaving you to question if or when you'll ever feel or be the same again.

As far as solutions go – everyone has an answer for you. Often, their well-intended solicitations only exacerbate the helplessness you experience. Infertility is not simple. It is a complicated and painful bind of wanting something so intensely but instead enduring repetitive efforts, recurring loss, trauma and painful waiting. You are constantly managing a host of other pressures that are often outside of your control. It is a journey that is difficult to put into words for those who haven't walked in your shoes.

You are in the middle of a heavy fog that changes your perspective on everything.

Physical, emotional, sexual, spiritual,
and financial aspects of one's life are all affected by this
disease of the reproductive system.[1]

– Windy Ezell, MA, LPC
www.innersolutionscounseling.com

The painful delays and complexities of infertility result in a total reorganization and reprioritization of your life – with or without your consent. These significant changes take place over time but are noticeably different and uncomfortable from the onset. You plan your life around what infertility demands and hope these many sacrifices and adjustments will pay off.

- Energy
- Time

- Focus
- Money
- Travel
- Schedule
- Sex Life
- Opportunities
- Relationships
- Faith and Religion
- Physical Comfort
- Psychological Comfort
- Constant Adaptation
- Future Planning
- Leisure Activities
- Alcohol and Diet
- Exercise Habits
- Hobbies
- Goals
- Work

With so many changes happening through infertility, Maslow's Hierarchy of Needs is one suggestion of the many as to how your basic needs may be reorganized. His motivation theory suggests that basic human needs are met in sequence, starting with the lowest tier, those of basic physiological needs.

If these are not met in sequence, your higher needs can suffer and go unmet. For example, infertility impacts your basic physiological need for health. So, according to Maslow's Hierarchy of Needs, an impact at the physiological level compromises your ability to feel safe and secure, to experience love and belonging. It also interferes with your ability to achieve self-esteem and create a self-actualized reality.

Infertility impacts daily choices, relationships, confidence, and your ability to live the fulfilled life you desire. Have you noticed a reorganization of your needs since infertility?

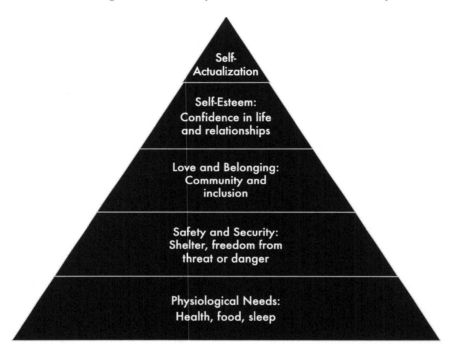

When you're focused on meeting
basic needs, you're in survival mode.
Everything else comes second.

Infertility requires that you shift gears to regulate and preserve energy in a new way. Everyday life can look and feel entirely different while in survival mode. It is important to recognize that during infertility you are fighting to meet your physiological need for health, which is the baseline for all your other needs.

Now more than ever you might question: 1) what you believe in and trust; 2) what you are capable of; and, 3) what your future goals will encompass. The infertility journey has many moving parts and constant highs and lows. Sometimes, you might be "all in," while at other times, you question everything and everyone -- including yourself.

- Can I handle this journey moving forward?
- Can I ever feel like the "old" me?
- Can I move my life to where I need it to be?
- Can I trust my judgment?
- Can I trust my body?
- Can I trust this process?
- Can I trust others?

It's okay to lean into this change. You are adapting. You are going through infertility to get through infertility. You are allowing these changes to occur so that hopefully, you may end these changes. You are in search of answers for yourself, and for your life.

Trust your judgement and decisions in this time. You will make it through. You will figure this out even though it might seem like there is no light at the end of the tunnel.

Staying connected with yourself at your core during this time is critical to rising above the challenges you're facing.

Positive affirmations are an important part of grounding yourself during unpredictable times. A recent brain-imaging study found positive neural brain changes in subjects who practiced self-affirmations focused solely on the future.[2] Self-affirming practices are also known to increase serotonin, the "feel good" hormone that regulates many physical functions including mood, appetite, sexual desire, digestion, and sleep.[3]

This means that by practicing positive self-dialogue during this time, you will help maintain your self-worth and personal confidence, as well as enhance how you feel every day.

Exercise

DAILY AFFIRMATIONS. Repeat these statements as often as you can throughout the day. Notice positive changes in your body.

- I am enough.
- I know what I'm doing, and I can trust my judgement.
- This is a painful season, but I can handle the feelings I'm experiencing.
- I know where I'm heading, even though I may be overwhelmed at times.
- I appreciate that I'm doing the best I can during this time.
- I trust that I can handle my future.
- I believe that my strength and courage are still here, allocated in new and different ways than before.
- I have confidence that I will figure out this area of my life.

CHAPTER 3:

TRAUMA 101

Trauma Afflicts

The beeping monitors synchronized as Karen gazed at the world outside her hospital room. Just one day earlier, she was looking through magazines, considering colors for the baby's room. Nothing could have prepared her for what was about to happen.

Years prior, Karen, a single mother by choice, began her fertility journey. It was a tough decision to do this by herself, but she couldn't tolerate the alternative of waiting any longer for that "special" someone.

She determined to "grab the bull by the horns" and do this process on her own. This choice resulted in both a profound grief over the loss of not having a partner, but also an equally intense dream of becoming a mother. With assisted reproductive treatment, she set out to accomplish all she intended and was loving her pregnancy as she entered her second trimester.

At week 20, during a routine prenatal checkup, Karen's dreams came crashing down. There was no heartbeat and an ultrasound confirmed that her baby had passed away days earlier. Karen was in shock. She had been so certain the pregnancy was safe, especially now that she was in her second trimester.

A trauma is a terrible and horrific event that you personally experience, witness, learn of, or discover. When a trauma occurs, you may feel helplessness, fear, and/or horror.

TRAUMA IS AN INESCAPABLE PART OF LIFE

In this world, trauma happens to everyone. Trauma affects each of us in a different and unique fashion. There is no right or wrong way to respond.

In 1997, Dr. Francine Shapiro presented two types of trauma: "Large-T" trauma and "Small-t" trauma.[1]

Large-T traumas are extraordinary events that can be life-threatening, result in serious injury, or threaten you or another's physical integrity. They cause severe psychological distress and helplessness because one cannot control or prevent the event. Psychological, cognitive, and physical sensations occur during these traumatic events. Daily functioning may be impaired. Such traumas may cause PTSD in some individuals.

Large-T trauma examples may include:

- Threats or actual serious injury and death
- Medical crises and surgeries
- Being a victim of robbery or another crime
- Community violence
- Chronic and repetitive experiences

- Child abuse
- Sexual violence
- Domestic violence
- Natural disaster
- Terrorism
- Presence in combat/war zone
- Car/plane accident
- School violence
- Refugee situations
- Captivity

Small-t traumas are overwhelming and highly distressing personal events that are non-life threatening. They do not impose any threat against physical integrity in the moment. Psychological, cognitive and physical sensations occur during these events, which may challenge your ability to cope and/ or cause significant emotional distress. Repeated exposure to Small-t traumas can be more harmful than experiencing a single, Large-T trauma, because the cumulative buildup of emotional suffering is complex.

Small-t traumas may include:

- Conflict with significant others
- Unprocessed traumas from the past
- Financial challenges and crises
- Neglect
- Social isolation
- Death of a pet
- Unemployment/job loss
- Legal issues

- Bullying
- Divorce
- Having an unsupported disability
- Discrimination

"Both big-t and small-t trauma deserve our attention. That is how they are resolved. We ignore this imbalance in our lives at a cost to our health and well-being, especially when their effects don't disappear. Both kinds are treatable, even when the trauma happened a long time ago or just yesterday. Mind and body deserve a break – treat them well."[2]

– Gail Johnson, LMSW, ACSW

When infertility occurs, it may present as either a Large-T or Small-t trauma. What determines the impact of infertility trauma for you is the result of several factors, including: the severity of the trauma, whether it is a single event or recurring one, and your unique beliefs, support systems, resources, core personal values, and expectations. Certain risk factors and precursors outlined below can also influence continued susceptibility to trauma:

- Close proximity to threat
- Chronic duration of trauma
- Early childhood trauma
- Inadequate social support
- Insufficient accessibility to professional support
- Existing mental health problems

The infertility trauma experience is often complex. For some, trying to conceive repeatedly and mourning each loss over and over produces a finite grief experience, like that experienced with a death, except the loss repeats. For others, enduring a miscarriage, ectopic pregnancy, in-utero loss and/or delivering a stillborn baby creates the death grief experience. For those who stop trying and remain involuntarily child-free, the same grief experience of a death may occur. Infertility "death" can be experienced in diverse ways, both figuratively and literally throughout many stages, changes to the plan, loss and challenging parts of the journey.

Trauma does not discriminate.
Infertility trauma hurts.

As trauma becomes more chronic and complex, you might find that separating from the grip and intensity of intrusive and repetitive thoughts becomes more challenging. You may struggle with powerful physical sensations and behaviors (anxiety, panic, nightmares, chronic pain, avoidance behaviors, and numbing, among others). Regulating past and present trauma can be an ongoing process.

"The weeks leading up to my thirteen-week pregnancy loss, I was blissfully unaware that anything could or would go wrong. In the ensuing months, I was anxious, depressed and isolated myself from family and friends and social events. My mind kept replaying the doctor's condolences of "I'm sorry, there's no heartbeat." I woke up each morning hoping that this was a nightmare.

When I got pregnant again, I struggled to stay positive that the pregnancy would remain viable. At the first ultrasound, my midwife took an agonizing amount of time finding the heartbeat, and I relived the moment I lost my baby. Tears of joy and relief followed when she finally found it.

It took until the twenty-week ultrasound to feel relatively confident that we would bring our baby home. I am now four years out, and there are still times that bring me back to that moment; passing by an ultrasound machine at my workplace, cleaning my closet and discovering the old ultrasound photos, or hearing of yet another pregnancy loss of a family member, friend, colleague, or patient. The trauma obviously remains in my body."

– Jen Noonan, MA, LPC
*In Due Time:
A Journey Through
Infertility, Loss, and
Embracing the Unknown*

According to Dr. William Tollefson, trauma impacts every part of the self and alters important aspects of human identity and personal philosophy.[3]

- Self-esteem
- Self-confidence
- Self-love
- Self-worth
- Individuality
- Personal Authority
- Qualities
- Traits
- Character

As you go through this journey, it's important to find space and respite apart from all these trauma demands. It may seem impossible, but you still need to find areas to exercise healthy control. You need to make as many daily life decisions as you can on your own terms. For example, setting aside dedicated time each day to meditate puts you in control of your schedule and self-care. Or, you might consider creating new goals involving education or travel. Such efforts can restore a sense of power and control that trauma steals.

You need that place or experience where you can just hit the "pause" button. And receive.

Exercise

GUIDED IMAGERY. This focused and directed form of meditation relies on the strength of your own personal imagination and relieves body and mind tension and pain.

Through audio visualization, one follows the speaker's lead and visualizes a different, comforting reality produced by one's own creative construction. Everything that creates distraction fades away into the background and full relaxation occurs.

Studies have shown that guided imagery helps to regulate cortisol and restore good balance.[4] Cortisol is a steroid hormone released during times of stress that plays a vital role in managing physical functions, including: regulating blood sugar levels, metabolism, and inflammation levels.[5] The benefits of guided imagery may include the improvement of your physical and psychological health.

Guided imagery programs are accessible at a number of websites, such as www.healthjourneys.com, and via the apps listed below. These can be used daily or as needed.

- Headspace
- FertiCalm
- Calm
- The Mindfulness
- Mindbody
- Circle + Bloom

CHAPTER 4:

TRIGGERS AND FLASHBACKS

"Traumatic memories are fixed and static.
They are imprints from past overwhelming experiences, deep
impressions carved into the sufferer's brain, body and psyche."

– Peter Levine, Ph.D.
Trauma and Memory: Brain and
Body in a Search for the Living Past

"Two years ago, we spent over a year going through two rounds of IVF. One year ago, we decided to take a break and stop all treatment. That meant no more appointments, and no more going to my clinic.

About six months ago, I needed to go back to my fertility doctor to have her remove some uterine polyps. But first, I had to have a preop appointment. That meant I would be going back to the fertility clinic for the first time in over a year.

What I didn't expect was to experience flashbacks just by being there.

As I waited in the room for my doctor I felt like my heart was going to beat out of my chest. I started to feel anxious as if my body was shutting down. I just wanted to get out of there. I thought back to all the time I had spent there doing IUI's and IVF and I felt hot and sweaty suddenly. Flashbacks.

As soon as my sweet doctor walked in the room I burst into tears. I didn't know why. I didn't know what was happening to me—but my body was reacting to all the trauma— emotionally and physically that I endured in that office.

My doctor was so kind and immediately acknowledged and validated that I had been through so much there that now it was all coming to the surface.

And then it clicked. Because of the PTSD I experienced because of Columbine, I realized that I too, was having PTSD symptoms related to infertility. It made sense."

– Cindy Maudsley, Columbine Survivor
*Cofounder of the blog, "Triumphs &
Trials" at www.triumphsandtrials.com
Founder of www.infertilitees.com*

A trigger is any event or experience involving touch, taste, sound, smell, sensation, or thought that awakens a memory and activates the emotions and behaviors experienced during that trauma.

In trauma, according to the mental health social network Psych Central, a trigger is, "Something that sets off a memory tape or flash back, transporting the person back to the event of her/his original trauma."[1]

Facts:

- Triggers from infertility trauma happen throughout a continuum of experiences and situations that are acutely painful reminders of loss.

- Triggers can be hard for you and those in your life to anticipate and understand.
- Sometimes you can make sense of the pain behind a trigger and sometimes you cannot. Either way, your body has stored a past memory that couldn't be experienced fully or processed at the time the event occurred.
- Your memory can retain information about trauma on a conscious and/or unconscious level.

Real or perceived threats that trigger a psychological response can surface in all kinds of places throughout the day. You might find that avoiding, managing, and planning for infertility triggers becomes a very consuming part of life. Understandably, you don't want to feel pain if you can avoid it.

You are hard wired to move toward what feels good and avoid what feels bad.

Trigger examples include:
- Family gatherings
- Phone calls/conversations
- Holidays
- Social media
- Health test results
- Fertility treatment(s)
- Spending money
- Planning
- Unexpected diagnoses

- Hospitals/clinics
- Ultrasounds
- Smells
- Calls from the doctor
- Friends with kids
- Menstrual cycle
- Waiting for answers
- Questions from others about children
- Bad news
- Surgeries and procedures
- Baby showers
- Birth announcements
- Shots and medication
- Relationship strain and conflicts
- Pregnant women
- Babies and kids
- Vacations
- Families
- Memories
- News stories

Triggers can leave you anxious, panicked, depressed, sad, fatigued, detached, and numb. Triggers can make you feel unsafe. They are stored in your mind and body on both conscious and unconscious levels.

1. **Conscious and expected trauma trigger –** In this instance, you are aware of the potential trigger and

make a conscious decision to either avoid the reminder altogether or manage the pain. For example:

- You make the conscious choice to skip a baby shower because you know it will be a trigger and cause pain.

- You get together with a group of friends who will be talking about their children at some point. You know it will trigger you but decide to go anyway.

2. **Unconscious and unexpected trauma trigger** – In this instance, the trigger catches you off guard. For example:

- A certain news story triggers unbearable sadness.

- A happy family with children next to you at a restaurant triggers your pain and grief.

- An impatient parent with their child triggers your anger.

With every trigger, it can seem as if you're losing control and power because you can't determine your fertility outcome. The reminders just keep coming. You might start avoiding people, events, and situations to control and manage triggers. Your personal boundaries can change over time. You may start to question your own judgment, limitations, and character.

Examples:

- Why can't I handle this?
- Is something wrong with me?
- Why don't I care anymore?
- Why am I feeling this way?
- Why don't I like this anymore?

- Why do I hate this now?
- Will I ever find comforting parts of my life again?
- How do I explain what I'm feeling?
- Why am I not a nice person anymore?
- Why can't I let it out?
- Why don't I feel like myself anymore?

According to Dr. Matthew Tull, many people with PTSD struggle to cope with flashbacks, which may occur as a result of encountering triggers.[2] A flashback is a sort of "re-experiencing" of a previous traumatic event.

"Flashbacks are like waking nightmares.
They are intense, repeated episodes of re-living the traumatic experience while you're fully awake. Flashbacks can come on suddenly and feel uncontrollable. They are more like a nightmare than a memory because sufferers often cannot distinguish between the flashback and reality, feeling like the traumatic experience is happening again, in the moment. Flashbacks are vivid, sensory experiences. During one, a sufferer might see, hear, and smell things they saw, heard and smelled during the traumatic moment."[3]

– Tiffany Chi, Contributing Author
www.talkspace.com

With a flashback, you may experience fear, horror, panic, rage, the need to escape, trembling, heavy breathing, dizziness, sweating and so on. Sometimes you understand the flashback and what it's tied to. In other situations, there are no answers on a conscious level.

Flashbacks are involuntary and intrusive reminders that don't require your consent. They can happen day or night. Flashbacks are exhausting and leave you depleted and tired.

There is hope.

One of the best ways to address triggers and flashbacks is to embrace compassion. First and foremost, it is important to know and acknowledge that you are not doing anything wrong. Disturbing memories are persistent and create intrusive symptoms. It takes a lot of emotional strength and stamina to repetitively experience the painful past.

Second, by kindly loving yourself during these episodes, you can more easily gather information and learn what your triggers are. Treat yourself with gentle care when triggers ignite shock, fear, loss, sadness, confusion, and a profound urge to escape. When a flashback occurs, remember that you are safe in the here and now. You can reduce the frequency of flashbacks by knowing your triggers.

Trigger Exercise

RAIN. You can ease trigger symptoms by using RAIN, a meditative approach that helps people connect, relate, manage, and ease difficult emotions. RAIN is a four-step coping method that was developed by mindfulness leader Michele McDonald roughly 20 years ago.

Notice what happens in your body with this practice.

Recognition. Recognize what is going on inside and around you. Ask probing questions such as, "What am I feeling and thinking? What is happening in my body right now?"

Get in touch with your whole mind and body experience and put a name to what you feel.

Acceptance. Accept and allow your experience in the moment. Even if it's not pleasant, let it be. Do not fight it or judge it. Say *yes* to whatever feelings you're observing. Remember that what you unconsciously resist or suppress persists and intensifies.

Interest. Gently explore what's happening inside. You might ask, "What part of me needs attention?" "Why am I feeling this way?" "What does this sensation in my body want from me?" "What am I saying or believing about the needs I have?" "How am I treating myself?"

Non-Identification. Allow yourself to have the thoughts and feelings that come with the trigger without letting them engulf or define you. Recognize you are safe in the here and now. This is a memory that is fleeting and will pass.

Flashback Exercise

FLASHBACKS. With flashbacks, practice grounding techniques to return your mind and body to the present moment and current reality.

- **Remind yourself that you're having a flashback.** Recognize that your brain is trying to process past traumatic memories.

- **Reframe your reality.** Remind yourself that the past is over and that you're safe now. You're in charge of this moment, time, and space.

- **Explore opportunities to activate and heighten the five senses (sight, sound, touch, taste, smell).**
  - → SIGHT: Walk around your home or office and count the number of lights.
  - → SOUND: Turn on music. Focus on the lyrics. Sing a song.
  - → TOUCH: Pour cold or hot water into your cup and focus on the temperature. Find an interesting texture and notice how it feels. Start coloring.
  - → TASTE: Eat anything you wish and focus on the taste.
  - → SMELL: Find a strong scent to inhale such as that of a candle, your favorite shampoo or essential oils.
- **Contact a friend or support person.**
- **Stand barefoot in the grass.**
- **Take a shower and alternate the temperature from hot to cold.**
- **Leisurely walk in the outdoors.**
- **Wrap up in a blanket.**

CHAPTER 5:

FIGHT, FLIGHT, OR FREEZE RESPONSE

Some responses are instinctual. You don't have to learn them.
They are already hard-wired to protect.

In the presence of a real or perceived threat, the primitive part of the brain takes over and moves your body into a protective state. It's all about survival.

Here's how it happens:

- When you perceive you are in danger, your brain sends a distress signal to the Sympathetic Nervous System.

- The body prepares to fight-or-flight from the perceived attack, threat, or harm.

- Stress hormones like adrenaline and cortisol are released throughout your body during this response, creating a sort of energy rush to prepare to fight or flee.

- This stress response continues until the perceived or actual threat is removed.

Other physical changes can occur during the fight-or-flight stress response such as:

- Muscle pain
- Shaking
- Insomnia
- Restlessness
- Panic
- Increased heart rate
- Abdominal discomfort
- Appetite changes
- Fatigue
- Hyperactivity
- Edginess
- Chills
- Change in body temperature
- Sweating
- Nausea or Diarrhea
- Feeling "out of it"

You may experience the fight-or-flight stress response throughout different points in the journey. Maybe it's waiting for results, a call from the doctor or a trigger – any of these and more could trigger your fight-or-flight stress response, depending on your perception of threat.

Fight-or-flight is designed to function in the short-term. It is intended to resolve any threat and move you away from danger, back to your baseline and normal state. That is the hope.

"The human brain has a safety switch that gets engaged by traumatic exposure and experiences. It's similar to being in shock but we remain there until it's long over. We detach. We create degrees of separation between ourselves and what we feel, think, perceive, and ultimately, this impacts not only our worldview but also our perception of self. Clinically, this is called 'Dissociation'."

– Jim LaPierre, LCSW
www.recoveryrocks.bangordailynews.com

Sometimes stress and trauma are so overwhelming that the fight-or-flight response just isn't enough. In this case, you cannot confront, nor can you flee the imminent danger. Like a deer in the headlights without any defense, your mind floods and you freeze. You dissociate – hoping to survive the threat.

Dissociation is both a coping skill and a defense mechanism during overwhelming trauma. Its purpose is to create a dividing line between you, the traumatic experience, and relevant memories.[1] Levels and symptoms of dissociation can vary widely from person to person, but typically increase during times of stress and prolonged trauma.

According to the International Society for the Study of Trauma and Dissociation, individuals struggling with dissociation encounter thoughts or emotions that seemingly come out of nowhere. "Typically, a person feels 'taken over' by an emotion that does not seem to make sense at the time.

Feeling suddenly, unbearably sad, without an apparent reason, and then having the sadness leave in much the same manner as it came, is an example. Or someone may find himself or herself doing something that they would not normally do but unable to stop themselves, almost as if they are being compelled to do it. This is sometimes described as the experience of being a 'passenger' in one's body, rather than the driver." [2]

Symptoms of dissociation/freeze include:

- Fatigue
- Anxiety
- Loss of focus
- "Blanked out" and dazed
- Depression
- A sense of detachment from others/self
- Memory loss or impairment
- Flashbacks
- Identity changes
- Feeling of detachment from others and self
- Suicidal thoughts
- Numbing
- Going "blank" for no apparent reason

There are many reasons why you might freeze/dissociate including:

- Continual stress is now the new normal.
- Your body has not received adequate time to recover after past trauma.

- It was a coping skill used in childhood that is now relied upon for everyday situations.
- Anticipation or imagination of future trauma or threats.
- In response to the perceptions of one or more of the five senses (sight, sound, touch, taste, smell), reminiscent of the original trauma.
- Involuntary thoughts and memories through flashbacks.
- Chronic depression and anxiety.
- Suicidal thoughts and actions.

In a chronic dissociated state, you can detach from everything - the good, the bad, and everything in-between.

If dissociation is persistent and recurring, treatment typically involves psychotherapy and sometimes medicine evaluation. Remember that during times of prolonged trauma, such as chronic infertility, dissociation levels may increase. Infertility trauma and resulting symptoms can be complex to manage, and difficult to understand in yourself and others. If you struggle with dissociation during this time, and it interferes with your daily functioning or relationships, consider speaking to a counselor for more support.

The infertility journey is unpredictable. It can wear you out and deplete your energy. The loss of control over your body is profound. At times, racing thoughts and unregulated physical and psychological sensations can leave you tired and drained, fearful, restless, angry, panicky, and confused. Your symptoms may vacillate daily. Some of the time you may have hyperarousal symptoms and operate in a high-anxiety state while other times you may be more prone to symptoms of depression, emotional numbing, withdrawing and dissociating from a reality that is too painful to bear.

In many cases of prolonged stress such as infertility, your nervous system can remain in overdrive from the fight, flight or freeze response which can result in dysregulation of your Sympathetic Nervous System (SNS) and your Parasympathetic Nervous System (PNS). Also understand that during chronic stress, your SNS dominates and suppresses vital functions of your PNS, which can impact how your body regulates anxiety and fear.

Sympathetic Nervous System (SNS)	Parasympathetic Nervous System (PNS)
Responsible for regulating fight, flight or freeze response.	Responsible for rest and digest function.
Responsible for producing energy for dire and/or urgent stress.	Responsible for healing and restoring the body.
Stimulating cortisol, adrenaline, and stress hormone production.	Responsible for supporting and repairing the body.

While it's important to rev up your engine for a crisis, you aren't meant to stay in the SNS. The PNS is the brake pedal that slows down or turns off an overactive SNS stress response.

Exercise

RESTORING PNS BALANCE. Your daily investment in your PNS can restore balance to your body that trauma disrupts. You can soothe and calm those internal emergency alarms by initiating more SNS activities such as:

- Art
- Meditation
- Prayer
- Low intensity exercise
- Progressive muscle relaxation
- Outdoor time
- Five sense activation – sight, sound, taste, touch, smell
- Diaphragm breathing
- Guided imagery
- Tai Chi
- Yoga
- Calming baths
- Binaural Beats Meditation
- Coloring
- Acupuncture and Massage Therapy
- Tension and Trauma Release Exercises TRE®

CHAPTER 6:

PTSD

"The threat is my body and mind."
– Anonymous

The helplessness from the loss of control over your body is profound. The recurring loss can create the potential for new trauma and PTSD. Research indicates that for those with PTSD, the continued exposure to cumulative and repetitive trauma creates greater distress than one single trauma.[1]

Karen was certain that it was just a matter of time before Erin would leave. It had been a hard and long couple of years. The pair's journey began years earlier when they made the choice to use a sperm donor. They were hopeful that with third-party reproductive assistance and IUI, Karen would become pregnant.

Over the last two years, the couple had completed six IUIs, none of which resulted in pregnancy. Additionally, Karen's mother had been diagnosed with cancer just one year earlier and her prognosis was now poor. Karen desperately wanted to have a baby and share this experience with Erin and her mother, but to no avail.

The urgency, pressure, and repetitive loss had overwhelmed Karen's ability to cope. She had more than reached her physiological threshold and could no longer tolerate the guilt and shame of not being able to conceive. She believed that somehow it was her fault and that she was letting everyone down. There was no rescue or relief from the pain of betrayal and rage she felt for her body.

She was either highly anxious or numbing and fatigued.

Karen didn't feel "right," or like herself anymore. She started having panic attacks and losing sleep. She detached from everyone including Erin, her mother, the rest of her family, community, and social circles. She didn't want to leave the house except for work. She now avoided the people and experiences she once loved. Erin didn't know how to support or reach Karen anymore. Their relationship and world together were falling apart.

"The avalanche. The free fall. The last step to the top of the mountain when things look beautiful and you can finally see over the hump (you made it – finally!), only to have the ground beneath your feet begin to move, tumbling out from under you, crumbling at your feet.

ROCK BOTTOM. I'm pretty sure that's where that terminology came from, because that's exactly what it feels like … like a thousand rocks just crashed down around you and you're buried far beneath the surface, not caring if anyone will ever find you.

If you've been there, you know it. It could be a failed IVF cycle … a failed surrogacy. It could be working for years to have a family unsuccessfully or finding out your child or family member has a critical health diagnosis. It could be a miscarriage … or an adoption that is cancelled. The loss of a child.

None of us expect these things to happen, and nothing can truly prepare us for when it hits."

– Christine Knapp, Blogger
www.ourbeautifulhope.com

Riding the infertility waves with circumstances vacillating daily is utterly exhausting at times. Furthermore, your investments don't guarantee a desirable outcome every time, which creates immeasurable pressures.

Unforeseen circumstances interfere and can bring "the plan" to an agonizing standstill. Menstruation arrives, and repetitive loss occurs. Trauma and PTSD can develop.

Posttraumatic stress disorder is a reaction to a past trauma. PTSD is a condition that can be diagnosed by a mental health professional when symptoms have lasted for at least one month following a trauma and those symptoms remain constant.[2]

Symptoms can develop immediately after a trauma event or appear later on at some future point. There are four main symptoms of PTSD:[3]

1. **RE-EXPERIENCING AND RELIVING THE TRAUMATIC EVENT**

   When any distressing recollection or memory of your trauma surfaces, you may re-experience and relive the traumatic event. Examples: trauma triggers, nightmares, flashbacks, rage, avoidance behaviors and acute anxiety sensations such as panic, sweating, and increased heart rate.

2. **AVOIDANCE**

   You may try to avoid activities, places, conversations, hospitals, locations, functions, activities, people, or any other triggers that remind you of the trauma. You may feel the urgency to escape certain situations now.

3. **NEGATIVE THOUGHTS AND MOOD**

   You might feel detached from yourself and others. You may find yourself losing interest in relationships and places that you enjoyed previously. Your mood may change and your overall outlook toward yourself, others, and the world can become more negative in general.

4. **INCREASED AROUSAL AND ANXIETY**

   With your body on "high alert," you may have trouble falling and staying asleep and/or you may struggle with nightmares. You may have difficulty concentrating or feel jumpy. You can become easily irritated, angered and startled.

Left untreated, PTSD symptoms may worsen, and functioning may become impaired.

There is growing research that points to infertility experiences resulting in PTSD for some, which emphasizes how important it is for those suffering to receive psychological support.

- Researchers found that four in 10 women reported experiencing symptoms of PTSD three months after their miscarriages or ectopic pregnancies.[4]

- Symptoms of PTSD have been described in both patients facing primary or secondary infertility who are undergoing or have completed infertility treatment.[5]

- A significant number of women who have experienced the trauma of stillbirth will be vulnerable to PTSD during a second pregnancy.[6]

- The results of one study indicated that advanced infertility treatment increases PTSD symptoms in medically diagnosed infertile women who do not receive psychological intervention throughout their treatment.[7]

Mind and Body Connection

The loss of control over your body and the infertility process can create a sense of profound physical abandonment. Before this season, you felt safe in your body – believing it would perform as you needed it to. Now, you're dealing with a different reality and a war rages between your mind and body. You might find yourself anxious, vulnerable/uncomfortable, and/or distrusting toward your body. This painful bind and body/mind conflict is referred to as Cognitive Dissonance. It is an internal tension that increases throughout infertility.

Mind	Body
I want this.	I am afraid of this.
I can do this.	I cannot handle this.
I can make this happen.	I am helpless.
I am moving toward this.	I want to move away from this.
I trust this.	I do not trust this.

Holding two opposite beliefs simultaneously is uncomfortable, sometimes unbearable. Daily, at times even hourly, it might seem one is caught in a rigorous mental ping-pong match trying to accommodate the constant flux of contradictory beliefs. Relief from this tension between your mind and body can't happen soon enough. Mindfulness practices reduce this tension and strengthen your ability to hold two opposing beliefs at the same time. These practices also help to reduce anxiety and hyperarousal in those with PTSD, as well as those with dissociative symptoms.[8]

"Mindfulness is the ability to develop acute and
sharp awareness of everything one does, which includes
the ability to catch the mind when it wanders, and the ability
to gently bring it back without making judgments
or criticisms about it."[9]

– Tatiana Santini, MA, RCC, RYT
www.truemind.ca

Dr. Alice Domar, Ph.D., a pioneer in the field of mind/body health, established the first Mind/Body Center for Women's Health, as well as the first Mind/Body Program for

Fertility.[10] A federally-funded research study revealed that 55% of women with infertility who consistently participated in Domar's Mind and Body Fertility Program were able to conceive within six months of participation, compared to the 20% in a control group who did not participate in any mind and body program.[11]

Research indicates that mindfulness practices align your mind and body to present time, place, and activity. When you can be present in the current moment in such a way that you are not overwhelmed or reactive to current reality, your self-trust and acceptance increase.

You are only responsible for right now,
today, in this very moment.
Nothing more is required from you.

Exercise

- Yoga
- Acupuncture
- Chiropractic care
- Massage therapy
- Guided-imagery
- Meditation
- Breathing practices
- Reiki and energy work

A CASE OF PTSD FROM PREGNANCY LOSS

– Lindsey M. Henke, MSW, LICSW

www.stillstandingmag.com

The "P" in my PTSD should stand for pregnancy loss, because pregnancy loss is what has created my posttraumatic stress syndrome. PTSD stems from the stillbirth of my daughter. I know outside of the loss community, people don't often want to hear about the trauma associated with the death of a child. Or, in the case of pregnancy loss, the trauma that we experience as our children are so confusingly born into this world yet have already died inside us.

Below are some of the criteria for PTSD with **my own personal experience added** to share with others how my PTSD is specifically shaped by pregnancy loss. Yours might look different.

Symptoms of **My** PTSD from Pregnancy Loss:

A. The person has been exposed to a traumatic event in which both the following are present:

1. The person experienced, witnessed or was confronted with a pregnancy that ended abruptly, never began or resulted in the death of the unborn child.

2. The person's response involved intense fear, helplessness or horror as s/he was forced to intensely participate in the birth of the dead child, which also resulted in the demise of his/her hopes and dreams.

B. The traumatic event is persistently re-experienced in one (or more) of the following ways:

1. Recurrent and intrusive distressing recollections of the delivery or loss of pregnancy and child.

2. Nightmares of the event or associated nightmares such as: of your husband/partner now dying, your dog dying, future babies you do not have dying, and horrific things happening that you did not dream of before the event.

3. Flashbacks to the moment when you heard the words, "No Heartbeat" and "I'm sorry your baby is dead" from doctors/nurses.

4. Intense psychological and physiological distress and reactivity at exposure to triggers from the event and reminders of not having the child you planned for (i.e., exposure to hospitals, living babies, pregnant women, the empty nursery, your own menstrual cycle and even car seats make your heart race.)

C. Persistent avoidance of stimuli associated with the trauma and emotional numbing including persistent symptoms of increased arousal (not present before the loss), such as:

1. Difficulty falling or staying asleep—Who sleeps well after knowing the worst can really happen to them and has?

2. Irritability—Having a short fuse because life has played a cruel joke on you.

3. Difficulty focusing—On anything but your own grief.

D. Duration of experience is more than one month—Yup! I have a feeling it will last a lifetime.

E. Causes clinically significant distress or impairment of everyday functioning—Yes! Your life is never the same, people at work think you should get over it but you can't focus, your relationship struggles in ways you never thought it would, and even doing a simple task like going to Target is impossible because you cry every time you walk by the baby section.

In conclusion, I think I have it! I have PTSD, but my "P" stands for pregnancy loss. I want readers to know that you can have PTSD (Post-Traumatic Stress Disorder) from a pregnancy loss, stillbirth, or the death of your child AND it's okay to seek help. I wrote this piece to let people see that even someone who is supposed to have her stuff together, as a mental health professional, can still get sideswiped by life and experience mental health struggles—like PTSD.

CHAPTER 7:

COMPLEX TRAUMA

"What happened to who you used to be? What happened to the person who believed in goodness, in safety, in connection, in your own confidence and self-efficacy, in your essential purpose and experience here on earth? Or, what happened to the person who believed in those things?"

– Michele Rosenthal, CPC, CH, NLP
Your Life After Trauma: Powerful Practices to Reclaim Your Identity

Complex-PTSD (C-PTSD) results from the long term psychological consequences of chronic inescapable trauma, over which a person has had minimal if any control.[1] The lack of safety during prolonged and repetitive traumas often creates intrusive PTSD symptoms and leaves many feeling lost and detached from their former selves.

With chronic infertility, you may feel helpless and trapped in an unending cycle of loss and trauma from a disease you can't control. You may experience a paradigm shift in your thoughts from this new world in which you live, that you feel lacks safety and reliability in many ways, including the following:

1. The trust in the goodness and fairness of the world is now gone or greatly reduced.

2. Your personal confidence is now changed. It's difficult to access those "safe" and "reliable" parts of your "pre-trauma" self.

3. You feel a loss over the ability to control your body and your life. Predictability is gone. It might seem there is no light at the end of this trial; you feel a desperate need to escape, to have this trial end.

4. If you can't fix it, maybe others can't either. The reliability of others and the world are now in question.

5. Between one loss and the next, there isn't the time and space needed for rest and recovery.

It's possible to have both PTSD and C-PTSD simultaneously.[2] While PTSD explains the dysregulation of symptoms resulting from trauma, C-PTSD explains more of the long-term impact of being traumatized repeatedly from an "inescapable" situation. Both have unique and separate features and characteristics.

PTSD	C-PTSD
Re-experiencing trauma in various ways	Identity changes
Avoiding reminders of trauma	Negative view of self and world
Increased anxiety	Difficulty regulating emotions
Rumination	Challenges with relationships
Flashbacks	Rage
Sleep disturbance, nightmares	Limited concentration
Easily startled, on guard	Severe body-image distortions
Waiting for the next "shoe to drop"	Chronic feelings of shame
Highly irritable	Distrusting of self/others
Detached and numb	Terror
Rage	Chronic feelings of helplessness
Negative mood	Dissociation

You can be an incredibly strong and resilient person, and still experience PTSD and C-PTSD from the complexities of infertility trauma.

If you're struggling with infertility, PTSD or C-PTSD, there's support for you. With the help of a counselor, strong community and network of support, you can learn to cope. Certain trauma-focused therapies and techniques address the many changing parts of trauma that can be difficult to understand and resolve on your own. Goals for both PTSD and C-PTSD therapy typically involve the following:

1. **Enhance safety and stabilization.** In this phase of counseling, you'll create a plan to stabilize your life. Trauma has stolen your sense of safety in yourself and the outside world. Over time, you'll develop needed internal resources and make the external adjustments to create safety again.

2. **Increase control.** You'll work to establish new ways to increase healthy physical and psychological control.

3. **Process trauma.** With the help of a professional, you can walk through traumatic events, grieve, and release the "frozen" PTSD symptoms from the past.

4. **Create a new connection with self.** You will focus on rebuilding your core areas of safety, security, and self-worth to restore what trauma took away.

5. **Focus on the present.** Because trauma creates strong fear circuits and physical memories, your therapist will focus on activities and treatments that help you retrain your brain and body to exist more cohesively in

the present moment. This will help you stop the cycle of vacillating between flashbacks and anticipation of future negative outcomes.

6. **Create a new normal.** This therapy phase explores the parts of you that have emerged and changed out of the trauma. It restores "wholeness" by integrating a life narrative (or explanation) of the past and present that provides some resolution, clarity, and purpose for future life chapters.

7. **Re-establish community and relationships.** Lastly, as you find like-minded people going through similar or the same struggles, you'll notice that you don't feel as isolated. Sharing the same goals, struggles, and feelings creates validation and promotes emotional health.

—— ❤ ——

"It appears the 3-month mark brings a resurgence of pain. So, it's the return of the sleeplessness and that heavy feeling on my chest, the one that makes it feel like I can't breathe. I think of how many times people say, 'how are you?' and how utterly impossible it seems to answer that question. There's no way to explain how I am with a quick answer; one you can give in the school playground while you wait for the bell to ring. What I'm going through right now is so beyond an easy pat answer to 'how are you doing?' I kept trying to find a word to describe how I was feeling. Then, it occurred to me: shattered.

In my mind I see someone picking up this beautiful priceless vase and violently throwing it on the ground. Now it's shattered in little pieces. The idea of leaving the pieces lying on the ground feels awfully tempting. Putting them back together seems like a daunting and impossible task. But the shattered pieces are more than just my life; they are my son, my marriage, my faith. So, I have no choice but to sit down in the middle of all the shards that are cutting me and making me bleed … and slowly and carefully and patiently put it back together again. And I know that no matter how carefully I put it back together, it will never be the same beautiful vase again. There will always be holes in the vase, in those places where the piece was simply too shattered to go back in. There will be weak places in the vase where if you press too hard the vase could shatter again. No, the vase will never be the same. Will it be beautiful in a different but special way? Will the glue that I use to painstakingly put it back together actually make it stronger? Will it still be able to hold water? I don't know the answer to any of these questions.

I know that I will spend the rest of my life periodically picking up the vase and seeing if I can put just one more piece in it, desperately trying to make it whole again. But, for today, I just sit in the midst of all the rubble and continue the agonizing task of putting it back together, one little piece at a time. And I know that I have to do it myself; no one can do it for me, in fact no one can even help me to do it. Although people can hold my hand or sit with me while I cry or bring me warm chocolate chip cookies, this is a task that only I alone can do.

People keep banging on the door screaming, 'Are you done yet?? Is it put back together yet?!' And I fear for the look on their faces when they finally see the vase and see that, no, it doesn't look the same, doesn't even look finished. It's different. And I fear even more the people who will look at the vase and see that it's different but not say anything; ignoring the fact that the vase has been changed forever, not acknowledging the tragedy that shattered the vase to begin with.

And I pray every day that God uses my hands to do this work. That He gives me strength and Grace, in both meanings of that word, to help me do what must be done. Grace is in every piece I put back together, in every drop of glue, in the essence of the vase. She is in the transformed beauty, she is in the strength, and most importantly, she is in the love that makes putting it back together my only choice."

— Judy, seven-year infertility survivor

Exercise

MOSAIC REFLECTION. Imagine that your life before infertility was a vase. One day a loss or trauma tips that beautiful vase to the ground. Tiny and large shards of glass are everywhere. What are you going to do with these glass shards? Will you simply discard them, or will you use them to create a new design and mosaic with the different sizes, shapes, and colors?

Consider buying a mosaic kit at the craft store to create a mosaic with awareness and intention. Allow yourself to create a design that reflects your inner experience. Upon completion, consider the following questions:

1. What do these pieces represent to you?
2. What do the colors and sizes say about you or your situation?
3. Is there any part of your design that "jumps out?" Anything that surprises you?
4. What does the way you've situated or placed the pieces together or apart represent?
5. What emotions can be attached to your mosaic design?
6. Does your mosaic represent parts of your past or hopes for the future?

CHAPTER 8:

PHYSICAL CHANGES

"The body of the traumatized individual refuses to be ignored."

– Babette Rothschild, M.S.W.
The Body Remembers

When the mind and body remain in "overdrive" for long periods of time, physical changes develop that can negatively impact mood and emotion, how a person feels about him or herself and others, and life productivity and satisfaction.

The initial physical changes that occur from trauma are immediate when the stress response (fight, flight, or freeze) is activated and releases cortisol, adrenaline, and other stress hormones into the body. These initial physical changes include:

- Pressure/heavy chest
- Abdominal issues: diarrhea
- Nausea
- Shaking/trembling
- Chills
- Racing heart
- Excess sweating

- Change in body temperature
- Lack of energy
- Insomnia
- Body aches, cramps, and pain
- Headaches
- Lightheadedness, fainting

Over the long term, intrusive and involuntary physical changes and symptoms will continually persist when trauma isn't resolved. Trauma experts believe the body retains these explicit memories on a cellular level—whether an individual consciously remembers them or not. The longer that trauma remains unresolved, the greater the risk for physical consequences that can include body tension, ailments, disease, chronic pain, and other health issues.

LIMBIC (BRAIN) CHANGES

In normal everyday situations, your brain can process information with ease. But when placed under the extreme psychological and physical conditions and pressures of a trauma experience, your brain can only process certain parts and fragments of the experience.[1] The remaining pieces of the trauma experience are stored in memories that are often "frozen" and tucked away into the unconscious. These unprocessed memories may surface at a later, "safer" time to be processed.[2]

Many who suffer with PTSD ask the following questions:
- Why can't I stop thinking about this?
- Why do I continue to have flashbacks?
- Why can't I turn my thoughts off?

With PTSD, the unresolved "stored" trauma memories continue to surface involuntarily through flashbacks, rumination, hyperarousal, nightmares, numbing, and avoidance behaviors. This often-confusing physiological process recurs until full resolution of trauma memories can heal and integrate. <u>Trauma symptoms can linger for years, waiting to be processed and healed.</u>[3]

Trauma creates brain changes, which is why telling someone with PTSD to just "get over it" or "move on" doesn't work.[4] The brain is not injured, but the brain has received new information from trauma and now regulates fear in a different way.

Trauma impacts your brain.

Today, neuroimaging studies are shedding light on significant brain changes that impact PTSD thinking and processing.[5] Common imaging scans used for these studies include magnetic resonance imaging (MRI), diffusion tensor imaging (DTI), positron emission tomography (PET), and single-photon emission computed tomography (SPECT).

Specifically, with PTSD, neuroimaging studies reveal brain volume and function changes.[6] Keep in mind, these changes can be reversed and rewired. The brain can recover.

1. HIPPOCAMPUS. Under normal circumstances, this part of the brain helps to distinguish between past and present experiences. It regulates memory, creating a story or narrative that places events in their right time and place.

Changes with PTSD:

- Smaller hippocampus.[7]

- Hippocampus can't regulate fragmented memories. It can't discern the past from the present, piece together memories, or create an integrated story.

- Triggers of the memory create ongoing flashbacks and involuntary, intrusive thoughts.

EXAMPLE: After loss and trauma, you're overwhelmed, scattered, and struggle to piece together what just happened. It can take a significant amount of time (even years) to fully absorb and piece together all the sequential moving parts of the trauma event. Unconscious stored memories surface through flashbacks, intrusive thoughts/ rumination and *felt* physical sensations—all contributing to the effort to be fully processed and placed in their right time and place.

2. AMYGDALA. Under normal circumstances, this part of the brain that helps with processing emotions is linked to fear responses. It discerns incoming threats, triggers, the fight-or-flight stress response, and signals when a threat is resolved.

Changes related to PTSD:

- A smaller amygdala is associated with greater vulnerability to having PTSD.[8]

- With PTSD, the amygdala remains hyperactive, even when there is no danger. It activates the fight-or-flight response, even when there is no danger.[9]

- Triggers of the trauma memory maintain the hyperactivity of the amygdala.

EXAMPLE: You learned of your miscarriage during an ultrasound. Time has passed and you're pregnant again. The nurse calls and it's time for another ultrasound. You panic. Your body is hyperalert and stressed from thinking about this appointment. In fact, at times, you feel like the loss is happening all over again, even though it seems this pregnancy is going well and there's no indication of problems.

3. PREFRONTAL CORTEX. Under normal circumstances, this part of the brain regulates emotional responses, impulses, behaviors, and fear.

   Changes with PTSD:

   - The prefrontal cortex is less active.[10]
   - The prefrontal cortex doesn't alert the amygdala to regulate fear properly nor does it challenge the hippocampus' fragmented narrative.
   - Increased rumination is connected to changes in the prefrontal cortex.

EXAMPLE: You've been invited to join your friends on a weekend getaway in a few months. Part of you desperately wants a change of scenery, but another part of you worries about coping, since they will discuss their children. You can't stop thinking about it, lose sleep, and ruminate for hours.

The importance of staying on top of the changes that have happened as a result of trauma cannot be underestimated. First, understanding what's happened to your brain validates why you think and feel the way you do. Second, it helps you to understand that you can rewire and change your brain.

1. With evidenced-based trauma therapies, memories of trauma that are stored in the brain and body can be released, reframed, and rewritten. This process offers significant physical and psychological symptom relief for individuals.

2. Mindfulness practices create positive brain changes. Empirical evidence shows that regular mindfulness practices change brain circuitry.[11]

3. Although the brain is not made of plastic, neuroplasticity refers to the adaptability and flexibility of your brain. It can be reorganized and rewired by creating new neuron and brain circuits. Everyday examples of neurogenesis include:

   • Physical exercise creates neuron growth in the brain.

   • New learning, such as taking on a new hobby or learning to play an instrument, improves memory function in the hippocampus and prefrontal cortex.

   • Changing basic daily routines creates new neural pathways.

ADRENAL CHANGES

"Numerous studies have already demonstrated that the chemical levels of adrenaline, cortisol, and serotonin in the body are significantly altered when individuals are exposed to prolonged or repeated experiences of trauma."

Dr. David Berceli
Trauma Releasing Exercises

Your adrenal glands assist with regulating hormonal balance by determining the amount of stress hormones to produce and distribute throughout your body. These hormones help stabilize mood and regulate stress.

Under normal circumstances, this process regulates with ease. But when stress and trauma are chronic, the demand for adrenaline increases while the production of serotonin, sometimes called "the happy drug," decreases. An exhausted and imbalanced adrenal system creates what many experts call "adrenal fatigue" or an "immune system collapse."

With overproduction of adrenaline and underproduction of serotonin, your body remains on high alert, even if it doesn't need to be. Changes may include:

- Easily startled
- Anger
- Rage
- Easily irritated
- Sensitivity to certain sounds, sights, smells, tastes, touch

This hormonal imbalance can also create more physical symptoms that are less noticeable and vary from person-to-person. Potential symptoms can include:

- Thyroid imbalance
- Low libido
- Arthritis
- Muscle weakness
- Nausea
- Blood pressure—high or low
- Loss of energy
- Premature menopause

- Polycystic ovary syndrome
- Poor egg health
- Sleep difficulty—falling asleep, staying asleep, sleeping too much
- Worsening of PMS symptoms
- Acne
- Depression
- Brain fog
- Anxiety or panic attacks
- Weight gain
- Caffeine dependence
- Intolerance to cold
- Irritable Bowel Syndrome
- Chronic anxiety
- Rage
- Hair loss
- Generalized chronic pain (fibromyalgia)

Exercise

If you suspect you may have physical symptoms due to trauma, consider speaking with your doctor so you can have diagnostic tests run and discuss treatment options to boost your immune system.

CHAPTER 9:

CONFIDENCE CRISIS AND IDENTITY SHIFTS

"Our doubts about our capacity to cope may cause a temporary diminishing of our self-esteem, just as certain uncomfortable feelings such as guilt or resentment cause us momentarily to feel badly about ourselves during the grieving process."

– Judy Tatlebaum, M.S.W., LCSW

The Courage to Grieve

John and Kari had been trying to conceive for more than two years, using an ovulation kit combined with homeopathic remedies. No pregnancy resulted, and this had taken a serious toll on their sex life. Fed up and discouraged, Kari finally called a reproductive endocrinologist and scheduled an appointment for fertility testing.

Days after meeting with the doctor, Kari received the test results and a recommendation that John come in for testing. John was shocked. Up until that point, he had silently blamed Kari for their issues. He had never even considered that he might not be able to pass on his DNA or help make a baby. This recommendation tugged at his pride and left him feeling a bit emasculated.

John's journey with grief had just begun as a semen analysis revealed that he had a very low sperm count. The news made him feel "less than" and inadequate as a man.

Finances were tight, and the prospect of undergoing surgery and IVF wasn't feasible at the time because their insurance would not cover such services. Kari wanted to borrow money from her family for fertility treatment, but John couldn't bear the thought of everyone knowing about their struggle—more specifically, his struggle. Kari was upset but tried to be supportive of his need for privacy.

John's utility was challenged, and he didn't know how to rectify the helplessness of this situation that created so much pressure. He now avoided sex as he didn't want to be reminded of what he couldn't provide. The shame and guilt were dominating the couple's relationship and eroding John's self-esteem and confidence.

Confidence is one of the primary and first casualties of infertility. You lose confidence in yourself, among other things. A survey of 585 men and women conducted in 2009 reported that seven in 10 women reported infertility made them feel flawed; half of the men reported infertility made them feel inadequate.[1]

When infertility is attributed to a male factor, in many cases, it presents a threat to the male partner's "manhood," self-image, and self-esteem.

Men derive so much of their identity from their ability to procreate that the male ego understandably tends to suffer when potency or motility issues prevent or threaten the lineage from being passed on.

Whether infertility is due to a male factor or not, men will often experience guilt as their wives or partners struggle physically. Sometimes helplessness sets in when men can't rectify the distressing situation. Historically society has taught men to be strong and tough, so even when a man is suffering emotionally, he may not want to burden his partner. Most men prefer to take the back seat emotionally and focus their attention on their partners during infertility. It is common for men to remain silent about their struggles.

Like the threat to manhood for men, women also doubt and question their womanhood during infertility. The dream of becoming a mother is often innate and developed years, sometimes decades, prior.

Many women desire to carry a pregnancy to full-term and have a biological child. When this desire is threatened, a woman may deem herself unworthy, incapable, and/or lacking as a "real" woman.

These losses can drive shame, embarrassment, and insecurity as well as a sense of feeling "flawed" or permanently damaged. Many women also derive significant life purpose from the role of motherhood. When this role is threatened, some women lose their sense of worth entirely. As time goes on, their insecurities will peak, and some will even question if their spouses will leave since they can't fulfill their "roles" or "duties" as a wife or partner.

The helplessness and powerlessness of infertility can impact self-image, self-esteem, and precipitate large amounts of shame. What you believed about yourself before infertility trauma can change after infertility has occurred.

BEFORE INFERTILITY TRAUMA	AFTER INFERTILITY TRAUMA
I can control/handle what I need to.	I have no control.
I am good enough.	I am not good enough.
I am adequate and capable.	I am inadequate and incapable.
I am in charge and make good decisions.	I don't trust myself.
I am strong.	I am weak.
I have choices.	I am powerless.
I have good physical health.	My body is permanently damaged.
I can protect myself from bad things.	I have no control. I am helpless.
I can fulfill my relationship duties.	I am failing my significant other.
I can get what I need and want.	I can't get what I need and want.

Infertility can challenge self-efficacy, a term that's used to describe the belief you have in your overall "effectiveness" as a person. You must be able to face difficult challenges and persevere to develop a strong sense of self-efficacy in life. Your response to difficult challenges defines how you will cope and weather the storm.

High self-efficacy thoughts can include:

- I can impact change.
- I can figure it out.
- I keep going no matter what.
- I adapt.
- I will work through it.
- I will make it work.
- I can own it.
- I will push through to the other side.
- I will master it.

In the daily infertility journey, you are moving your way into the future you want and desire. You're aligning your energies, time, and resources to support your goals. Do you trust yourself? Have you lost sight of the remarkable person you are or the strength of your capabilities? Trauma can create subtle yet profound confidence shifts, detachment from yourself and others, and impact your overall perception of self.

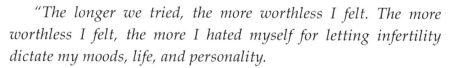

"The longer we tried, the more worthless I felt. The more worthless I felt, the more I hated myself for letting infertility dictate my moods, life, and personality.

As time ticked on, more and more of my friends got pregnant without drama. This of course made me feel even worse. I grew jealous, impatient, and bitter. I started throwing daily pity parties. I played my favorite game, "Why them? Why not me?" which made me even more reclusive. I disappeared from Facebook. I sunk into my bed. I watched a lot of Netflix. I couldn't deal with anyone who was happy or well-adjusted or confident. I only wanted to be around other self-loathing, depressed people. Or (preferably) no people at all.

I've never felt worse about myself than I did those first two years battling infertility. All the bad breakups, pimples, final exams, hungover mornings, bad decisions, and embarrassing moments combined didn't make me feel half as worthless as my infertility did. I felt defective. Like I just wasn't willing my ovaries into submission hard enough. Like they were dogs that just needed to be trained to ovulate.

The worst part? I could feel my personality shifting underneath me, like some emotional tectonic plates. And I hated it. Who was I if I wasn't the brash, strong, creative, confident woman asking for what she needed? I hated this new turn my personality was taking...this woman was not me. And this self-loathing made me retreat even further into myself.

A thought I kept returning to was: if a relatively well-adjusted, confident, outgoing woman like myself was reacting this way to infertility, what havoc was it wreaking on quieter, more emotionally vulnerable women? What were they going through? How was this changing them? How was this affecting their lives, friendships, and marriages?"

Elyse Ash, Founder of Fruitful Fertility *www.fruitfulfertility.org*

The loss of control during infertility trauma can be so sudden and severe that it breaks a core trust within you. Identity shifts can happen when you don't feel safe, secure, or comfortable inside your own body or feel unable to control or manage the trauma that creates unrelenting circumstances to endure.

"A main factor in how you define yourself is the context in which you understand where and how you belong. Naturally your identity has changed since your trauma(s), because your understanding of who you are and the world in which you live has dramatically changed."

– Michele Rosenthal, CPC, CH, NLP
Your Life After Trauma: Powerful Practices to Reclaim Your Identity

It can be helpful to identify and name the many vacillating parts of change that can happen during infertility. Shifts in everyday reality can impact your identity and sense of self.

Are you experiencing any of the following shifts?

1. **Trouble discerning what's going on inside your body.** You may not feel "right," and, in response to these uncomfortable feelings, experience flashbacks or chronic anxiety.

2. **Implemented changes in boundaries.** With trauma triggers and reminders of loss, you might avoid certain places, people, or anything reminiscent of the trauma.

3. **Experienced sexuality under fire.** Meaningful sex is now replaced with ambivalent scheduled meetings in the bedroom. Sex has become a burden and leads to resentment as well as deep insecurity in yourself and/or your partner.

4. **Struggled with sleep disturbances and insomnia.** These create daily fatigue as well as mood and personality shifts.

5. **Sensed a "lack of belonging."** You can't relate to others and feel cut off from social circles. You isolate.

6. **Faced challenges with your significant-other relationship.** Resentments, anger, and defensiveness overwhelm former ways of coping with hardship and issues together.

7. **Detached from yourself.** You feel numb or just zone out. You struggle with depression or dissociation. Staying grounded in the present is now difficult.

8. **Irritated more than usual.** Anger, nervousness, irritability and rage result from trauma and PTSD. Your body remains on "high alert" when there is no threat or danger in the present moment. Fight, flight, or freeze reactions are magnified in comparison to before.

9. **Struggled with physical changes**. Weight gain, pelvic pain, bloating, dizziness, and a host of other changes can trigger the "loss of control" feelings.

10. **Faced hormonal imbalances from treatments.** You may experience side effects of moodiness, irritability, fatigue, reduced sex drive, and weight gain.

11. **Frightened by parts of life**. The things you used to enjoy trigger anxiety now. The world doesn't feel safe or predictable anymore.

No matter where you find yourself at this time, know that you will create a new normal again. Author and professional trauma coach Michele Rosenthal provides a solid understanding and roadmap for rebuilding your life after trauma in her book, *Your Life After Trauma: Powerful Practices to Reclaim Your Identity.* Consider educating yourself about this process when you are ready and be sure to access the *Resources* section in the back of the book.

Exercises

So that you can gain back the confidence, self-appreciation, and admiration that you once had, you need to recognize where you've been, how hard you're working and what you're truly capable of.

1. **Positive remembering.** Write down as many memories and situations you can recall where you felt competent. As you spend time doing this, notice what's happening in your body.

2. **Thought Log Record.** This is a cognitive behavioral therapy (CBT) tool that addresses the way you believe.

Use the daily record below to identify and log anything that triggers painful emotions, feelings, uncomfortable physical sensations, thoughts, and/or behaviors.

Examples:

1. **Situations** – Had a flashback of miscarriage
2. **Thoughts** – My body is permanently damaged
3. **Emotions** – Sad, fear, shame
4. **Behavior** – Binged on food or spending

Then, challenge these thoughts and behaviors with alternative thoughts such as:

- "My body is safe now. That was then, this is right now."
- "My body is strong. I am strong. I can handle this."

If you get stuck, consider the following questions about your thoughts:

- Are they true?
- If your best friend/partner/spouse said this about her/himself, what would you say?
- Is this helpful to you?
- Do you have evidence of what you're telling yourself?
- Is there something that can contradict these thoughts?
- What do you need and want to hear instead?

With repetitive cognitive restructuring, new thoughts align with *who you really are*, and there will be a noticeable difference between old and new thinking.

Example:

- **Old Thinking:** I can't do this. I don't have what it takes. I'm going to fail again. I can't handle this. I can't have what I need. They don't think I can do this. I failed the last time. I'm not sure I'll make it. I'm not enough. I'm inadequate.
- **New Thinking (Alternate Thoughts):** I have this. I can have what I need. I will make it. I will knock this out. I will nail this down. I can and will do this. I can

handle this. I can trust myself. I can be proud of myself. I can believe and trust in myself. I can take good care of myself. I'm enough. I'm adequate.

3. **Compassion letter.** With compassion, write a letter to your future self. Write about what you're going through and learning in the present. Write about what you hope for, what your goals are, and what is helping you in the present.

CHAPTER 10:

GRIEF

Hope deferred makes the heart sick.

– Proverbs 13:12 (NIV)

For many, traumatic grief inevitably visits at some point during infertility. Not being able to procreate isn't something you just "get over" or "snap out of." In fact, traumatic grief is often a prolonged process because of the major life disruption the loss creates. It adds one more emotional mountain to climb in your life when resources are already limited from being in survival mode. The depth and physiological complexity of your grief can feel insurmountable at times.

The isolation and silent struggle of infertility additionally compounds grief, which can drive shame, dread, fear, loneliness, jealousy, rage, denial, anger, panic, sadness, terror, bargaining, and/or depression.

Your grief demands answers. Why did this happen? How can this be prevented? In search of explanations, answers and meaning, a subtle or profound paradigm shift takes place in your thoughts. Some questions you might be asking yourself are:

- Am I safe?
- Is my body safe?
- Are others safe?
- Is the world safe?
- Is it safe to trust God?
- Can I meet my own needs?
- Can I count on others?
- Are my needs legitimate?
- Am I worthy of good things?
- Am I loveable as I am?
- Am I good enough?
- Is something wrong with me?
- Am I shameful?
- Am I permanently damaged?
- Am I adequate?
- Have I done everything I should?
- Have I done something wrong?
- Should I have known better?
- Who is responsible for this?
- Is this my fault?
- Am I in control?
- Am I powerless and helpless?
- Can I make this happen?
- Can I handle this?
- Why can't I control my emotions?

Your thoughts and beliefs about yourself, others and the world can drastically change after loss. Perhaps life doesn't make sense anymore. Your heart is broken, and infertility has disrupted the deepest surface and direction of your life. Grief is now part of the journey, it can't be avoided.

Grief is a normal reaction to loss. However, sometimes grief is misunderstood. Others might communicate concern for your grief and recovery process. You might wonder if your experience is normal. Rest assured, there is no right or wrong way to grieve. Everyone has a unique grief response, and you have a right to your own individual experience.

Exercise

JOURNALING. Much evidence suggests that journaling provides amazing health benefits, including strengthened immune function, drops in blood pressure, and improvements to sleep patterns.[1] Because grief can produce complicated emotions, journaling can offer a place to fully express yourself, speak your truth with total acceptance and process your feelings.

The Center for Journal Therapy recommends the following five "WRITE" steps for daily journaling:[2]

W – What do you want to write about? What's going on? How do you feel? What are you thinking about? What do you want? Name it.

R – Review or reflect on it. Close your eyes. Take three deep breaths. Focus. You can start with "I feel..." or "I want..." or "I think..." or "Today...." or "Right now..." or "In this moment..."

I – Investigate your thoughts and feelings. Start writing and keep writing. Follow the pen/keyboard. If you get stuck or run out of juice, close your eyes and re-center yourself. Re-read what you've already written and continue writing.

T – Time yourself. Write for 5-15 minutes. Write the start time and the projected end time at the top of the page. If you have an alarm/timer on your PDA or cell phone, set it.

E – Exit smart by re-reading what you've written and reflecting on it in a sentence or two: "As I read this, I notice—" or "I'm aware of—" or "I feel—." Note any action steps to take.

Used with permission from Kathleen Adams LPC, Center for Journal Therapy, *www.journaltherapy.com*.

CHAPTER 11:

CHOICES

The challenge is learning to trust oneself to make the best choices along the way, despite the constant ambiguity during infertility.

Infertility isn't your choice. It can be painfully complex and confusing at times. And, the choices you must make during this season are not always black and white. There is no "one way" or "right path" to choose, which complicates the journey even more.

For those who ask the question, "When should I (we) stop trying?" -- there is no right or wrong answer. Ultimately your response and decisions are yours to make and should be honored and respected by friends, family, medical experts, and social circles.

If you're currently traumatized and struggling, the subject of choice might create a painful and overwhelming discussion. On one hand, you want to end the impact and risk of recurrent trauma and pain. But continued internal conflicts ensue around desires and wants, and so before you know it, the discussion is back on the table once again. At other times, you may be considering the choice to stop trying altogether and remain involuntarily child-free or create your family alternatively.

With PTSD, the discussion of personal choices itself can trigger a traumatic response of acute anxiety, flashbacks, rage, negative mood, helplessness and physical symptoms. You're wanting to avoid anything and everything reminiscent of the trauma(s) including discussions of choices related to infertility. But at the same time, you feel an undeniable sense of urgency to face and implement choices.

New and emerging negative beliefs can surface in consideration of the revolving infertility choices:

- I can't trust myself.
- I can't trust others with decisions.
- I don't know what I'm doing.
- I feel shame.
- I am permanently damaged.
- I can't handle this.
- I can't get what I need or want.
- I have nothing to look forward to.
- I can't handle my life.
- I don't deserve to be happy.
- I don't deserve good things.

The conversation of choices becomes forced as infertility was never in the plan and now produces hurt, loss, and grief. Exercise self-compassion, validation, and self-acceptance as you examine choices.

Exercise

Recognize that making choices during this time is difficult. Consider the following thought-provoking activities.

1. **Refuel.** What are you doing to refuel during this season? What is your plan? Are you pushing yourself too hard? Have you created a good balance?

2. **Shift the internal dialog.** What are you telling yourself? Change the internal dialogue to a positive affirming statement. Practice often.

   - I am enough as I am.
   - I can figure out my life.
   - I deserve a good life.
   - I can trust my judgment.
   - I know what I'm doing.
   - I am doing the best I can.
   - I am worthy and honorable.
   - I can take good care of myself.

3. **Incentivize and reward.** If you're going to move in a direction that increases risk and potential pain, strategize rewards. What does your courage equal? What can you consider to increase comfort in this high time of vulnerability? Plan a mini getaway, eating at your favorite restaurant, buying that ____, and so on. Reward your efforts, regardless of the outcome.

4. **Set tentative deadlines.** Setting deadlines for yourself provides psychological benefits, especially during infertility. The deadlines you set are not fixed and can be revisited and adjusted at any time.

   Deadlines:

   - Create movement.
   - Create clarity and structure.
   - Enhance personal vision.

- Allow you to plan.
- Enhance your sense of control.
- Validate your process and decisions, creating normalcy in what you're doing and why.

5. **Recognize the emotional push/pull process.** During infertility, sometimes you're "all in," other times, you're "all out." Be aware that this is a very normal response cycle in unpredictable situations.

6. **Accept that pain is part of the process.** Whatever path you choose, recognize that there could be pain involved. It can't be avoided. Remember that you are equipped and able to handle any future challenges and can seek out support if needed.

7. **Ask for expert advice.** Gathering different medical viewpoints, diagnoses, and knowledge can provide insight and perspective that can help you navigate the decisions ahead.

8. **Consider all your options.** The more choices you can explore to fulfill your dream or life, the less pressure just "one" outcome will entail.

9. **Create supportive alliances and community.** Having a network of friendships and backing from individuals in infertility support groups can help you through this time. Refer to the *Resources* section in the back of the book for more information on support communities.

10. **Take a break if needed.** Although you may experience both pros and cons from taking time off, sometimes the space and structure that a "time-out" provides is invaluable. It can be the perfect respite for recharging and rebooting your life emotionally and physically.

CHAPTER 12:

THE VILLAGE

"If a lonely person is able to make one more friend, the loneliness starts to diminish. All sorts of scary things become possible when you have a friend to do them with."

Jacqueline Olds, MD
& Richard S. Schwartz, MD
The Lonely American (2008)
[Reprinted with permission,
Beacon Press, Boston, MA]

"Isolation was one of the most difficult parts of infertility that I encountered throughout my journey. Yes, the countless doctors' appointments, needles, blood draws, injections as well as the weight gain and roller coaster of emotions had their fair share of difficulty as well, but it was the feeling of being alone that really stung.

I know that I was not totally alone as I walked through the infertility path of my life... First, my husband was nothing less than amazing throughout all of this. From day one. He always has been and continues to be my rock. He was suffering himself and was so, so, so gracious to put my feelings before his own. He told me all the time that his job was to be the positive one. He said that I could do the crying and have the anger; he would have the good thoughts—enough for both of us. I love him for that more than I can express in words. It brings tears to my eyes when he told me that God's plan was for us to find each other for a reason, and perhaps all of this is part of that reason, regardless of how it would pan out. Second, I know that I had my family. They didn't always know what to say (and that's OK!), but they knew how to listen (really well!) and when to embrace me just when I needed those welcoming arms of comfort (whether in-person or over the phone), they even know how to help me to think outside of the box (thanks, Mom!)...but that said, even with all the love and support of those around me, infertility still caused me to feel isolated...Isolated from the world, really."

– Aubrey Exarhos, Blogger
www.blogger.com

During infertility, isolation and loneliness may become a way of life for you. Your former community may no longer offer the same meaning, safety and support it once did. And, while some relationships may withstand the whirlwind of infertility, others won't -- despite the love and care that may exist on all sides. Your instinct may be to retreat and withdraw from connections and relationships to protect yourself against reminders, conversations, and realities that are painful.

"Everywhere you turn, pregnant mothers, children, babies, and families, exacerbate the painful exclusion and feelings of stigmatization, ostracizing, and judgment.
Isolation hurts."

– *Anonymous*

Although protecting yourself is a natural defense and survival mechanism, it can create more loneliness and isolation if you don't form and establish new connections.

- Research and neuroimaging studies indicate that pain resulting from exclusion and social rejection is experienced as real, physical pain.[1]

- Research also shows that having social support available during socially painful situations reduces the amount of that physical pain and one's susceptibility, and, that resiliency significantly depends on the amount of social support and number of connections a person has.[2,3]

- Another study showed that women who developed social networks through which they could disclose and process their journeys, experienced greater quality of life during infertility.[4]

You need your village.

Having others to talk with about the experiences you are facing and knowing you aren't alone in your struggles, can provide you with a real sense of safety and comfort. Your social network should include those who truly understand your journey, who can provide validation and support your process.

Do you have enough support? Have your relationships suffered from infertility? Finding social networks and maintaining or developing new relationships is an important step toward avoiding isolation. You aren't meant to go through this alone, and many infertility organizations and resources exist to help you connect to others in this time.

Think about your current village and the family and friends who existed long before infertility.

- Are you receiving the support you need?

- Are you telling your friends and family about your difficulties with conceiving?

- Are you comfortable when they ask about your process?

- Do you feel your village understands what you're going through?

Exercise

Consider writing a letter to friends and family. Jody Earle of Freeville, New York developed one in her work, "Infertility: Helping Others Understand – A Guide for Family and Friends," which is included below. Use or modify her letter, presented here with permission, for friends and family. If you don't want to send a letter, consider writing a letter anyway for the therapeutic relief that comes from owning your story and validating the experience.

Sometimes your words will strengthen your strongest fortress.

Dear Family and Friends,

*I want to share my **feelings** about infertility with you, because I want you to understand my struggle. I know that understanding infertility is difficult; there are times when it seems even I don't understand. This struggle has provoked intense and unfamiliar feelings in me and I fear that my reactions to these feelings might be misunderstood. I hope my ability to cope and your ability to* *understand will improve as I share my feelings with you. I want you to understand.*

You may describe me this way: obsessed, moody, helpless, depressed, envious, too serious, obnoxious, aggressive, antagonistic, and cynical. These aren't very admirable traits; no wonder your understanding of my infertility is difficult. I prefer to describe me this way: confused, rushed and impatient, afraid, isolated, and alone, guilty and ashamed, angry, sad and hopeless, and unsettled.

*My infertility makes me feel **confused**. I always assumed I was fertile. I've spent years avoiding pregnancy and now it seems ironic that I can't conceive. I hope this will be a brief difficulty with a simple solution such as poor timing. I feel confused about whether I want to be pregnant or whether I want to be a parent. Surely if I try harder, try longer, try better and smarter, I will have a baby.*

*My infertility makes me feel **rushed and impatient**. I learned of my infertility only after I'd been trying to become pregnant for some time. My life-plan suddenly is behind schedule. I waited to become a parent and now I must wait again. I wait for medical appointments, wait for tests, wait for treatments, wait for other treatments, wait for my period not to come, wait for my partner not to be out of town and wait for pregnancy. At best, I have only twelve opportunities each year. How old will I be when I finish having my family?*

*My infertility makes me feel **afraid**. Infertility is full of unknowns, and I'm frightened because I need some definite answers. How long will this last? What if I'm never a parent? What humiliation must I endure? What pain must I suffer? Why do drugs I take to help me, make me feel worse? Why can't my* body do the things that my mind wants it to do? Why do I hurt so much? I'm afraid of my feelings, afraid of my undependable body and afraid of my future.

My infertility makes me feel **isolated and alone**. Reminders of babies are everywhere. I must be the only one enduring this invisible curse. I stay away from others, because everything makes me hurt. No one knows how horrible is my pain. Even though I'm usually a clear thinker, I find myself being lured by superstitions and promises. I think I'm losing perspective. I feel so alone, and I wonder if I'll survive this.

My infertility makes me feel **guilty and ashamed**. Frequently I forget that infertility is a medical problem and should be treated as one. Infertility destroys my self-esteem and I feel like a failure. Why am I being punished? What did I do to deserve this? Am I not worthy of a baby? Am I not a good sexual partner? Will my partner want to remain with me? Is this the end of my family lineage? Will my family be ashamed of me? It is easy to lose self-confidence and to feel ashamed.

My infertility makes me feel **angry**. Everything makes me angry, and I know much of my anger is misdirected. I'm angry at my body because it has betrayed me even though I've always taken care of it. I'm angry at my partner because we can't seem to feel the same about infertility at the same time. I want and need an advocate to help me. I'm angry at my family because they've always sheltered and protected me from terrible pain. My younger sibling is pregnant; my mother wants a family reunion to show off her grandchildren and my grandparents want to pass down family heirlooms. I'm angry at my medical caregivers, because it seems that they control my future. They humiliate me, inflict pain on me, pry into my privacy, patronize me, and sometimes forget who I am. How can I impress on them how important parenting *is to me? I'm angry at my expenses; infertility treatment is extremely expensive. My financial resources may determine my family size. My insurance company isn't cooperative, and I must make so many sacrifices to pay the medical bills. I can't miss any more work, or I'll lose my job. I can't go to a specialist, because it means more travel time, more missed work, and greater expenses. Finally, I'm angry at everyone else. Everyone has opinions about my inability to become a parent. Everyone has easy solutions. Everyone seems to know too little and say too much.*

*My infertility makes me feel **sad and hopeless**. Infertility feels like I've lost my future, and no one knows of my sadness. I feel hopeless; infertility robs me of my energy. I've never cried so much nor so easily. I'm sad that my infertility places my marriage under so much strain. I'm sad that my infertility requires me to be so self-centered. I'm sad that I've ignored many friendships because this struggle hurts so much and demands so much energy. Friends with children prefer the company of other families with children. I'm surrounded by babies, pregnant women, playgrounds, baby showers, birth stories, kids' movies, birthday parties and much more. I feel so sad and hopeless.*

*My infertility makes me feel **unsettled**. My life is on hold. Making decisions about my immediate and my long-term future seems impossible. I can't decide about education, career, purchasing a home, pursuing a hobby, getting a pet, vacations, business trips and houseguests. The more I struggle with my infertility, the less control I have. This struggle has no timetable; the treatments have no guarantees. The only sure things are that I need to be near my partner at fertile times and near my doctor at treatment times. Should I pursue adoption? Should I take expensive drugs? Should I pursue more specialized and costly medical intervention? It feels unsettling to have no clear, easy answers or guarantees.*

Occasionally I feel my panic subside. I'm learning some helpful ways to cope; I'm now convinced I'm not crazy, and I believe I'll survive. I'm learning to listen to my body and to be assertive, not aggressive, about my needs. I'm realizing that good medical care and good emotional care are not necessarily found in the same place. I'm trying to be more than an infertile person gaining enthusiasm, joyfulness, and zest for life.

*You can **help me**. I know you care about me and I know my infertility affects our relationship. My sadness causes you sadness; what hurts me, hurts you too. I believe we can help each other through this sadness. Individually we both seem quite powerless, but together we can be stronger. Maybe some of these hints will help us to better understand infertility.*

*I need you to **be a listener**. Talking about my struggle helps me to make decisions. Let me know you are available for me. It's difficult for me to expose my private thoughts if you are rushed or have a deadline for the end of our conversation. Please don't tell me of all the worse things that have happened to others or how easily someone else's infertility was solved. Every case is individual. Please don't just give advice; instead, guide me with your questions. Assure me that you respect my confidences, and then be certain that you deserve my trust. While listening try to maintain an open mind.*

*I need you to **be supportive**. Understand that my decisions aren't made casually, I've agonized over them. Remind me that you respect these decisions even if you disagree with them, because you know they are made carefully. Don't ask me, "Are you sure?" Repeatedly remind me that you love me no matter what. I need to hear it so badly. Let me know you understand that this is very hard work. Help me realize that I may need additional support* *from professional caregivers and appropriate organizations. Perhaps you can suggest resources. You might also need support for yourself, and I fear I'm unable to provide it for you; please don't expect me to do so. Help me to keep sight of my goal.*

*I need you to **be comfortable** with me, and then I also will feel more comfortable. Talking about infertility sometimes feels awkward. Are you worried you might say the wrong thing? Share those feelings with me. Ask me if I want to talk. Sometimes I will want to, and sometimes I won't, but it will remind me that you care.*

*I need you to **be sensitive**. Although I may joke about infertility to help myself cope, it doesn't seem as funny when others joke about it. Please don't tease me with remarks like, "You don't seem to know how to do it." Don't trivialize my struggle by saying, "I'd be glad to give you one of my kids." It's no comfort to hear empty reassurances like, "You'll be a parent by this time next year." Don't minimize my feelings with, "You shouldn't be so unhappy." For now, don't push me into uncomfortable situations like baby showers or family reunions. I already feel sad and guilty; please don't also make me feel guilty for disappointing you.*

*I need you to **be honest** with me. Let me know that you may need time to adjust to some of my decisions. I also needed adjustment time. If there are things you don't understand, say so. Please be gentle when you guide me to be realistic about things I can't change such as my age, some medical conditions, financial resources, and employment obligations. Don't hide information about others' pregnancies from me. Although such news makes me feel very sad, it feels worse when you leave me out.*

*I need you to **be informed**. Your advice and suggestions are only frustrating to me if they aren't based on fact. Be well* informed so you can educate others when they make remarks based on myths. Don't let anyone tell you that my infertility will be cured if I relax and adopt. Don't tell me this is God's will. Don't ask me to justify my need to parent. Don't criticize my course of action or my choice of physician even though I may do that myself. Reassure yourself that I am also searching for plenty of information which helps me make more knowledgeable decisions about my options.

I need you to **be patient**. Remember that working through infertility is a process. It takes time. There are no guarantees, no package deals, no complete kits, no one right answer, and no "quickie" choices. My needs change; my choices change. Yesterday I demanded privacy, but today I need you for strength. You have many feelings about infertility, and I do too. Please allow me to have anger, joy, sadness, and hope. Don't minimize or evaluate my feelings. Just allow me to have them and give me time.

I need you to **be strengthening** by boosting my self-esteem. My sense of worthlessness hampers my ability to take charge. My personal privacy has repeatedly been invaded. I've been subjected to post-coital exams, semen collection in waiting room bathrooms, and tests in rooms next to labor rooms. Enjoyable experiences with you such as a lunch date, a shopping trip, or a visit to a museum help me feel normal.

Encourage me to maintain my sense of humor; guide me to find joys. Celebrate with me my successes, even ones as small as making it through a medical appointment without crying. Remind me that I am more than an infertile person. Help me by sharing your strength.

Eventually I will be beyond the struggle of infertility. I know my infertility will never completely go away because it will *change my life. I won't be able to return to the person I was before infertility, but I also will no longer be controlled by this struggle.* **I will leave the struggle behind me**, *and from that I will have improved my skills for empathy, patience, resilience, forgiveness, decision-making and self-assessment. I feel grateful that you are trying to ease my journey through this infertility struggle by giving me your understanding.*

** Jody struggled with infertility for 11 years and had three pregnancy losses, one during each trimester, and had two live births of premature sons who are now healthy young men.

CHAPTER 13:

PRACTICES AND TREATMENT

"I have learned that no matter what culture, language or psychosocial background, all humans have an innate capacity to heal from traumatic experiences."

– Dr. David Berceli
Trauma Releasing Exercises

The people who have the greatest capacity to recover from traumatic experiences and PTSD are those who are willing to learn about their symptoms and explore all their options for implementing a compassionate plan of action for their own recovery process.

There is no one-size-fits-all approach. Instead, most individuals use a combination of techniques and interventions with the support of a licensed mental-health therapist and/ or physician. Whatever combination you choose, stay as proactive as you can in the practices of your approach.

Before you begin, speak with your physician to explore what treatment, approaches and frequencies are best for where you're at right now.

TRAUMA-BASED THERAPIES

Every individual will have a unique treatment plan. If you have trauma and PTSD, you may want to consider evidence-based, trauma-informed therapy. These therapies are specifically developed to address trauma, among other issues, and will help you understand how trauma impacts your emotions and behaviors. These therapies are helpful for reducing PTSD symptoms.

Evidence-based, trauma-informed therapies are those that integrate *"clinical expertise, patient values, and the best research evidence into the decision-making process for patient care."*[1]

Examples include:

1. Eye-Movement Desensitization and Reprocessing (EMDR)

   - EMDR therapy has been around since the late 1980s, when it was developed by Dr. Francine Shapiro. This therapy is extensively researched and practiced worldwide. It is noninvasive and has proven effective for treating trauma and reducing distressing symptoms.

   - EMDR allows individuals to process the trauma memory in a noninvasive approach with combining a bilateral stimulation action (a backand-forth pattern) using touch, sight or hearing devices.

   - You can locate an EMDR therapist via a Google search or at *www.emdr.com.*

2. Prolonged Exposure Therapy (PE)

- Decades of research have proven that PE, which was developed by Edna B. Foa, Ph.D., reduces PTSD symptoms.

- PE is a type of cognitive behavioral therapy that helps individuals process their memories of trauma through gradual exposure and movement toward the very memories, feelings, and stimuli that have been avoided since the trauma.

- The more the trauma is talked about and not avoided, the more a patient desensitizes the overwhelming experience and the more likely it is that fear is reduced.

- You can locate a PE therapist via a Google search.

3. Cognitive Processing Therapy (CPT)

- Developed in the 1980s by Drs. Patricia Resick, Candice Monson, and Kathleen Chard, CPT has proven to be an effective treatment for PTSD and other symptoms that develop in the aftermath of trauma.

- CPT is a type of cognitive behavioral therapy that helps individuals identify belief changes (safety, trust, etc.) impacted by the trauma. It teaches individuals how to challenge and change beliefs about the trauma that are no longer helpful. CPT uses writing and homework assignments that facilitate trauma processing.

- You can locate a CPT provider via a Google search.

TRAUMA-BASED PHARMACOLOGY

Research has shown that pharmaceuticals are another option for treating PTSD and trauma symptoms. However, some of these, such as antidepressants and antipsychotics, may impact fertility and pregnancy. These are risks that you'll want to consider and discuss with your doctor.

MIND AND BODY PRACTICES

After loss and trauma, the anxiety about past events and anticipated future scenarios can become overwhelming. When your body remains in a constant state of hyperarousal, more stress hormones are produced, which can impact ovulation, reduce libido for both men and women, and reduce sperm count in men, not to mention a host of other physical and psychological symptoms.

During infertility and PTSD, it is important to develop a regular routine of activities that strengthen your mind to increase body health, while also reducing anxiety and stress. Mind-body practices can include meditation and acupuncture. Additional examples are listed below in the *Exercise* section for this chapter. These practices allow you to separate and disconnect from stimuli and outside stress that might otherwise vie for your attention.

The bottom line is that trauma recovery is a process of releasing the intensity and grip of intrusive and involuntary psychological and physical symptoms. When you're in the "thick of it," recovery may seem like an unreachable goal because you are just trying to survive.

Don't give up! Remember that as you learn to understand what is happening between your body and mind and strengthen that connection, you will more easily be able to find comfort in the present moment and manage trauma symptoms more easily.

Exercise

These mind and body practices can be implemented in the comfort of your own home with instructional videos or using downloaded applications; they also can be implemented in-person by a trained practitioner:

- Acupuncture
- Restorative and other different types of yoga
- Massage therapy
- Fertility Pilates
- Guided imagery
- Tension and Trauma Release Exercises TRE®
- Chiropractic and osteopathic care
- Biofeedback
- Prayer
- Relaxation and breathing exercises
- Journaling
- Tai Chi and Qigong
- Aromatherapy
- Positive affirmations
- Emotional freedom technique (EFT)
- Reiki/energy work

CHAPTER 14:

SELF-CARE

"The most powerful relationship you will ever have is the relationship you have with yourself."

– Steve Maraboli
www.stevemaraboli.net

You need you—now more than ever. Loss experienced in the past or loss anticipated in the future can be draining and all-consuming, both emotionally and physically. Your mind and body may feel pulled from all sides, but you are having a normal reaction to trauma.

Be extra good to yourself in this time, pay close attention to what you need and give accordingly. Nurture self-connection, self-love and activities that comfortably attach you to your core. Practice regular self-care to stay grounded in present day levels of safety, worthiness, control, and comfort.

Consider the following questions as you consider your present needs vs. coping skills in this time.

- Am I getting enough sleep, exercise, and nutrition?
- What people or activities in my life are helping me? What is hindering me?

- What allows me to feel good about myself?
- What experiences increase comfort in my body?
- What do I need? How can I give this to myself?
- What gives me joy?
- What makes me laugh?
- Who are my people?
- Do I have enough support?
- What makes me feel safe?
- What makes me feel grounded?
- Am I being gentle with myself or pushing myself too hard?
- Do I need a break? If so, am I giving myself one?
- Am I engaging in any leisure activities? What do I need in this area?
- Am I setting good limits with others where I need to?

As you consider what type of self-care you need in this time, recognize that the coping skills you had before infertility may need to change now. Perhaps they don't work the same anymore, or you are limited in what you can do now because of treatments and other facets of this journey. Maybe you need different outlets for managing stress now.

Now is the time to focus on you. As your time and energy demands increase through infertility, it is critical to stay on top of self-care.

Determine to make a customized self-care plan. Put a list on your calendar or make a list to remind yourself of what you need so that *you* stay the priority.

Exercise

SELF-CARE. In survival mode, your focus and energies change. Consider and rate the following self-care questions to assess all areas in this time – physical self-care, psychological self-care, emotional self-care, spiritual self-care, and professional self-care. Consider any other needs you have that may not be included in this list.

The following self-care worksheet is simply a suggestion.[2] Feel free to add to or modify it.

From Transforming The Pain: A Workbook On Vicarious Traumatization by Karen W. Saakvitne Laurie Anne Pearlman. Copyright © 1996 by the Traumatic Stress Institute/Center for Adult & Adolescent Psychotherapy LLC. Used by permission of W. W. Norton & Company, Inc.

Rate the following areas using this scale:

How well are you doing with self-care?

5 = Frequently

4 = Occasionally

3 = I barely or rarely do this

2 = I never do this

1 = This never occurred to me

Physical Self-Care

_____ Eat regularly (e.g., breakfast, lunch, dinner)

_____ Eat healthily

_____ Exercise

_____ Get regular medical care for prevention

_____ Get medical care when needed

_____ Take time off when sick

_____ Get massages

_____ Dance, swim, walk, run, play sports, sing, or do some other fun physical activity

_____ Take time to be sexual - with myself, with a partner

_____ Get enough sleep

_____ Wear clothes you like

_____ Take vacations

_____ Take day trips or mini-vacations

_____ Make time away from telephone

_____ Other:

Psychological Self-Care

_____ Make time for self-reflection

_____ Have my own personal psychotherapy

_____ Write in a journal

_____ Read literature that is unrelated to work

_____ Do something at which you are not expert or in charge

_____ Decrease stress in my life

_____ Engage my intelligence in a new area, e.g., go to an art museum, history exhibit, sports event, auction, theatre performance

_____ Practice receiving from others

_____ Be curious

_____ Say no to extra responsibilities sometimes

_____ Other:

Emotional Self-Care

_____ Spend time with others whose company you enjoy

_____ Stay in contact with important people in your life

_____ Give yourself affirmations, praise yourself

_____ Love yourself

_____ Reread favorite books, re-view favorite movies

_____ Identify comforting activities, objects, people, relationships, places and seek them out

_____ Allow yourself to cry

_____ Find things that make you laugh

_____ Express your outrage in social action, letters, donations, marches, protests

_____ Other:

Spiritual Self-Care

_____ Make time for reflection

_____ Spend time with nature

_____ Find a spiritual connection or community

_____ Be open to inspiration

_____ Cherish your optimism and hope

_____ Be aware of nonmaterial aspects of life

_____ Try at times not to be in charge or the expert

_____ Be open to not knowing

_____ Identify what is meaning to you and notice its place in your life

_____ Meditate

_____ Pray

_____ Sing

_____ Have experiences of awe

_____ Contribute to the causes in which you believe

_____ Read inspirational literature (talks, music, etc.)

_____ Other:

Workplace or Professional Self-Care

_____ Take a break during the workday (e.g., lunch)

_____ Take time to chat with co-workers

_____ Make quiet time to complete tasks

_____ Identify projects or tasks that are exciting and rewarding

_____ Set limits with clients and colleagues

_____ Balance your caseload so no one day or part of a day is "too much"

_____ Arrange your work space so it is comfortable and comforting

_____ Get regular supervision or consultation

_____ Negotiate for your needs (benefits, pay raise)

_____ Have a peer support group

_____ Develop a non-trauma area of professional interest

_____ Other:

Balance

_____ Strive for balance within your work-life and workday

_____ Strive for balance among work, family, relationships, play, and rest

Outline other areas of self-care that are important and/or relevant to you.

CHAPTER 15:

FOR FAMILY AND FRIENDS

The effect you have on others is invaluable.

The psychological and physical consequences of infertility are no doubt far reaching, not only for those going through infertility but also for their family and friends. Loss and change can be painful for those who are in your corner and grieving in their own way for you, with you, and for the dream you (and they) wish for.

It can be hard for all invested or involved parties during infertility. Some family and friends can easily manage and support each other throughout turbulent seasons, while others struggle to navigate the inevitable painful changes from differentiation in experiences and coping styles that become apparent and often magnified throughout.

Without walking in your loved one's place, it is difficult to understand what he or she is truly facing. Many facing infertility have difficulty putting their experience into words for someone who has not experienced the same overwhelming journey.

If you are reading this book to learn more about infertility and PTSD, perhaps you simply want to understand a loved one better and learn how to most effectively support him or her during this time.

RESOLVE, the National Infertility Association, has developed infertility etiquette advice and important tips on how to help a friend or family member struggling with infertility:

1. **Don't tell the person to relax.** Infertility is a medically diagnosable condition for which relaxing is not a cure. Telling someone to relax during infertility is incredibly painful.

2. **Stay informed and educated.** If you don't understand what your friend or family member is facing, ask them to share education and information so that you can walk alongside them with compassion and support. That goes a long way.

3. **Be open to change.** Be sensitive to what your friend or family member needs during this time and respond with care.

4. **Don't minimize the problem.** Do not explain why the glass is half-full to those facing infertility or the "benefits" of their situation.

5. **Don't ask why they aren't trying IVF or considering adoption.** Whatever choices they make is the result of an often complicated and painful process. Offering unsolicited insight or guidance can exacerbate their grief and undermine their confidence.

6. **Don't treat them like they're ignorant.** They are well informed and know what they are doing. Treat them as the expert(s) on their own journey.

7. **Don't complain about your own pregnancy.** Be sensitive to those around you and their painful journey of trying to conceive or produce a sustained pregnancy.

8. **Don't say there are worse things that could happen.** Just as you would not want to be invalidated during a personal crisis, consider that infertility may be the most painful experience your friend or family member has ever experienced.

9. **Let them know that you care.** Just letting them know you care and can be relied upon -- if needed -- for support.

10. **Support any decision to stop treatment.** If one is made, support the decision to stop treatments, whether you understand or support their reasons or not. Once people have closed certain chapters, don't keep asking them to reopen them. Respect their process toward closure.

PTSD can also create significant and painful relationship changes that are difficult to understand. There are ways to support them during these changes.

1. **Don't pressure them.** Don't pressure them into speaking to you or a professional about their struggles. Just let them know you are there to be supportive, that will go a long way. If they want to speak to you or someone else at some point, they will.

2. **Plan fun and meaningful activities.** Help create new memories. Help them experience life apart from their trauma experience. Plan a hike, go for a drive, or try a new restaurant.

3. **Plan for triggers.** Become familiar with your loved one's triggers—conversations, activities, and anything that creates a painful reminder and/or flashback. In doing so, you can support, validate, and respect their needs during these instances.

4. **Educate and inform yourself about PTSD.** There's a plethora of education that can be found in media sources today outlining PTSD, its symptoms, and what to expect.

5. **If you are currently pregnant or become pregnant and have been a support person, understand that sensitivity and extra consideration go a long way.** Consider ways to communicate the information that minimizes hurt such as writing a letter, so that the person experiencing infertility can have safe space to be vulnerable and experience what they need to.

6. **Don't talk someone out of their feelings.** Whether or not you agree with them about their fears, understand that PTSD is an anxiety disorder with physiological symptoms that do not heal overnight. Understand that infertility is a unique and arduous experience; do not deny them their right to feel as they do.

7. **Believe them.** Don't play devil's advocate or invalidate their experience. You do not have to understand what they're facing, but you can trust that they do and just support them in their perception of their experience.

Change is painful because it requires movement by one or both parties in relationships. It means that what "was" in the relationship is no longer. It means that boundaries and needs are changing. You can move out of your comfort zone and adapt to these changes or possibly lose more.

If you're struggling to work through these changes or support your loved one, consider speaking with a specialist or counselor. Visit some of the professional organizations online (listed in the *Resources* chapter) that provide education, tips and tools related to infertility for the general public.

RESOURCES

As you continue your journey in life and continue to heal from infertility, trauma, and PTSD, consider the following books, national organizations, and online resources to support you in your process. Continue the process of pacing yourself and keep in mind that reading any of the listed materials could trigger your history of trauma so be sure to stop reading if the material isn't helpful. Continue at your own pace if it is.

Infertility Resources:

1. The World Health Organization (WHO) is a United Nations agency dedicated to International Public Health. www.who.int/en/

2. The Centers for Disease Control and Prevention is a science-based organization that provides important health information and data for the United States. www.cdc.gov/reproductivehealth/infertility

3. The American Society for Reproductive Medicine is a non-profit organization providing education and multidisciplinary standards for reproductive medicine. www.asrm.org

4. RESOLVE: The National Fertility Association provides education, advocacy and community resources for anyone challenged in the area of family building. www.resolve.org

PTSD Resources:

1. www.healmyptsd.com
2. www.ptsdalliance.org
3. www.apa.org/topics/ptsd
4. www.sidran.org

RECOMMENDED READING

1. Berceli, David. (2015). *Trauma releasing exercises: A revolutionary new method for stress and trauma recovery.* USA: TRE.

2. Domar, Alice. (2002). *Conquering Infertility. Dr. Alice Domar's Mind/Body Guide to Enhancing Fertility and Coping with Infertility.* New York, NY: Penguin Books.

3. Levine, Peter A. (1997). *Waking the tiger: Healing trauma.* Berkeley, CA: North Atlantic Books.

4. Naparstek, Belleruth. (2014). *Invisible heroes: Survivors of trauma and how they heal.* New York, NY: Bantam Dell.

5. Rosenthal, Michele. (2012). *Before the world intruded: Conquering the past and creating the future.* Palm Beach Gardens, FL: Author.

6. Rosenthal, Michele. (2015). *Your life after trauma: Powerful practices to reclaim your identity.* New York, NY: W.W. Norton & Company.

7. Rothschild, Babette. (2000). *The body remembers: The psychophysiology of trauma and trauma treatment* (1st ed.). New York, NY: W. W. Norton & Company.

8. Shapiro, Francine. (2012). *Getting past your past. Take control of your life with self-help techniques from EMDR therapy.* New York, NY: Rodale.

9. Schwartz, Arielle. 2016. *The complex PTSD workbook: A mind-body approach to regaining emotional control and becoming whole.* Berkeley, CA: Althea Press.

10. Tolle, Eckhart. 2004. *The Power of Now: A Guide to Spiritual Enlightenment.* Novato: Namaste Publishing and New World Library.

REFERENCES

Introduction

1. American Psychiatric Association. (2013). *Diagnostic and statistical manual of mental disorders* (5th ed.). Washington, DC: Author.

Chapter 1

1. World Health Organization. (WHO). (n.d.). *Sexual and reproductive health: Infertility is a global issue.* Accessed March 10, 2018. Retrieved from http://www.who.int/reproductivehealth/topics/infertility/perspective/en/

2. World Health Organization (WHO), & The World Bank. (2011). *Disabilities and rehabilitation; World report on disability.* Retrieved from http://www.who.int/disabilities/world_report/2011/report/en/

3. RESOLVE: The National Infertility Association. (2018). *Infertility FAQ.* Retrieved from https://resolve.org/infertility-101/infertility-faq/

4. Center for Disease Control and Prevention, National Center for Health Statistics. (2016). *Infertility.* Retrieved from https://www.cdc.gov/nchs/fastats/infertility.htm

5. Diamond, R., Kezur, D., Meyers, M., Scarf, C., & Weinshel, M. (1999). *Couple therapy for infertility.* New York, NY: Guilford Press.

6. Harvard Health Publishing. Harvard Medical School. (2009, May). *The psychological impact of infertility and its treatment* [Newsletter]. Retrieved from https://www.health.harvard.edu/newsletter_article/The-psychological-impact-of-infertility-and-its-treatment

7. Harvard Health Publishing. Harvard Medical School. (2009, May). *The psychological impact of infertility and its treatment* [Newsletter]. Retrieved from https://www.health.harvard.edu/newsletter_article/The-psychological-impact-of-infertility-and-its-treatment

8. Domar, A. D., Zuttermeister, P. C., & Friedman, R. (1993). The psychological impact of infertility: A comparison with patients with other medical conditions. *Journal of Psychosomatic Obstetrics and Gynaecology, 14,* 45-52. Retrieved from https://www.ncbi.nlm.nih.gov/pubmed/8142988

9. Wolff Perrine, J. (2010, August 5). Many couples struggle with infertility in silence. *Self.* Retrieved from http://www.nbcnews.com/id/38311820/ns/health-womens_health/t/many-couples-struggle-infertility-silence/#.WqRYlujwaUl

10. Fike, M. (2015, January 13). I thought having a baby when I was 'ready' would be easy. I was wrong. *The Guardian*. Retrieved from https://www.theguardian.com/commentisfree/2015/jan/13/having-a-baby-ready-easy-wrong-infertility

11. Fike, M. (2017, December 6). What to expect when you're… Still not expecting. *Huffington Post*. Retrieved from https://www.huffingtonpost.com/monica-fike/what-to-expect-when-youre-trying-to-expect_b_9643242.html

12. Hope, M. (2016, August 24). Six infertility bloggers explain what infertility feels like [Blog post]. Retrieved from http://itspositiveliving.com/ infertility-bloggers-explain-infertility-feels-like/

Chapter 2

1. Ezzell, W. (2016). The impact of infertility on woman's health. *North Carolina Medical Journal, 77*(6), 427-428. doi:10.18043/ncm.77.6.427

2. Cascio, C. N., O'Donnell, M. B., Tinney, F. J., Lieberman, M. D., Taylor, S. E., Strecher, V. J., & Falk, E. B. (2015). Self-affirmation activates brain systems associated with self-related processing and reward and is reinforced by future orientation. *Social Cognitive and Affective Neuroscience, 11*(4), 621-629. doi:10.1093/ scan/nsv136

3. McIntosh, J. (2018, February 2). What is serotonin and what does it do?. *Medical News Today*. Retrieved from https://www.medicalnewstoday.com/kc/serotonin-facts-232248

Chapter 3

1. Marich, J. (n.d.). What are adverse life experiences?. *Gracepoint: The Source for Wellness*. Retrieved from https://www.gracepointwellness.org/109-post-traumatic-stress-disorder/article/55727-what-are-adverse-life-experiences

2. Johnson, G. G. (2017, February 8). Big "T" vs. little "t" trauma [Blog post]. Retrieved from https://www. shirleyvalk.com/blog/big-t-vs-little-t-trauma

3. Tollefson, B. (2013, January 19). Trauma robs you of your identity [Blog post]. Retrieved from http://williamtollefsonvalues.blogspot.com/2013/01/loss-of-identity-to-trauma.html

4. Jones, D., Owens, M., Kumar, M., Cook, R., & Weiss, S. M. (2014). *Journal of the International Association of Providers of AIDS Care (JIAPAC), 13*(4), 318-323. doi:10.1177/2325957413488186

5. What is cortisol?. (n.d.) *Hormone Health Network*. Retrieved from https://www.hormone.org/hormones-and-health/hormones/cortisol

Chapter 4

1. University of Alberta, Sexual Assault Centre. (2016, July 17). What is a trigger?. Retrieved from https://psychcentral.com/lib/what-is-a-trigger/

2. Tull, M. (2008, October 29). PTSD: Coping with flashbacks. The Path Home: Veterans Helping Veterans and Their Families. Retrieved from http://www.thepathhome.net/p-t-s-d-.html

3. Chi, T. (2017, June 26). What happens in your brain during a PTSD flashback? Retrieved from https://www.talkspace.com/blog/2017/06/happens-brain-ptsd-flashback/

Chapter 5

1. Tracy, N. (2017). What is dissociation? Definition, symptoms, causes, treatment. Retrieved from https://www.healthyplace.com/abuse/dissociative-identity-disorder/definition-of-dissociation-symptoms-causes-treatments/

2. Dissociation FAQ's. (n.d.). International Society for the Study of Trauma and Dissociation. Retrieved from http://www.isst-d.org/?contentID=76

Chapter 6

1. Karam, E. G., Friedman, M. J., Hill, E. D., Kessler, R. C., McLaughlin, K. A., Petukhova, M., . . . & Koenen, K. C. (2014). Cumulative traumas and risk thresholds: 12 month PTSD in the world mental health (wmh) surveys. *Depression and Anxiety, 31*(2), 130–142. doi10.1002/da.22169

2. Symptoms of PTSD. (n.d.). Anxiety and Depression Association of America. Retrieved from https://adaa.org/understanding-anxiety/posttraumatic-stress-disorder-ptsd/symptoms#

3. American Psychiatric Association. (2013). *Diagnostic and statistical manual of mental disorders* (5th ed.). Washington, DC: Author.

4. Farren, J., Jalmbrant, M., Ameye, L., Joash, K., Mitchell-Jones, N., Tapp, S., . . . & Bourne, T. (2016). Post-traumatic stress, anxiety and depression following miscarriage or ectopic pregnancy: A prospective cohort study. *BMJ Open, 6*(11). doi10.1136/bmjopen-2016-011864

5. Rettner, R. (2012, August 8). Fertility treatment puts women at risk of stress disorder. *Live Science.* Retrieved from https://www.livescience.com/22194-fertility-treatment-ptsd.html

6. Turton, P., Hughes, P., Evans, C. D. H., & Fainmain, D. (2001). Incidence, correlates and predictors of

post-traumatic stress disorder in the pregnancy after stillbirth. *The British Journal of Psychiatry, 178*(6), 556-560. doi:10.1192/bjp.178.6.556

7. Corley-Newman, A. (2016). *The relationship between infertility, infertility treatment, psychological interventions and posttraumatic stress disorder* (Doctoral dissertation). Walden University, Minneapolis, MN. Available at http://scholarworks.waldenu.edu/ dissertations/2805/

8. Boyd, J. E., Lanius, R. A., & McKinnon, M. C. (2018). Mindfulness-based treatments for posttraumatic stress disorder: A review of the treatment literature and neurological evidence. *Journal of Psychiatry and Neuroscience, 43*(1), 7–25. doi:10.1503/jpn.170021

9. Santini, T. (2014). *The importance of mindfulness, self-compassion, and yoga in healing trauma* (master's thesis). Adler Graduate School of Minnesota, Richfield, MN. Available at http://www.academia.edu/7017628/ The_Importance_of_Mindfulness_Self-Compassion_ and_Yoga_in_Healing_Trauma

10. Alice Domar, Ph.D. (n.d.). About Alice Domar, Ph.D. Domar Center for Mind/Body Health. Retrieved from https://www.domarcenter.com/about/staff/ alice_domar

11. Program Benefits. (n.d.). The mind body program for fertility. Domar Center for Mind/Body Health. Retrieved from https://www.domarcenter.com/ mind-body/programs/

Chapter 7

1. Post-Traumatic Stress Disorder. (n.d.). Mental Health America. Retrieved from http://www.mentalhealthamerica.net/conditions/post-traumatic-stress-disorder

2. Post-Traumatic Stress Disorder. (n.d.). Mental Health America. Retrieved from http://www.mentalhealthamerica.net/conditions/post-traumatic-stress-disorder

Chapter 8

1. Berceli, D., (2005). *Trauma releasing exercises: A revolutionary new method for stress/trauma recovery* (p. 40). Charleston, SC: Create Space Publishers.

2. Berceli. D., (2005). *Trauma releasing exercises: A revolutionary new method for stress/trauma recovery* (p. 40). Charleston, SC: Create Space Publishers.

3. Green, M. (2017, March 23). A radical new therapy could treat the 'untreatable' victims of trauma. *Newsweek*. Retrieved from www.newsweek.com/2017/03/31/trauma-ptsd-therapy-comprehensive-resource-model-treats-untreatable-572367.html

4. Rosenthal, M. (2018). The science behind PTSD symptoms [Blog post]. Retrieved from https://psychcentral.com/blog/the-science-behind-ptsd-symptoms-how-trauma-changes-the-brain/

5. Holzschneider, K., & Mulert, C. (2011). Neuroimaging in anxiety disorders *Dialogues in Clinical Neuroscience, 13*(4), 453–461. Retrieved from

https://www.researchgate.net/
publication/221776054_Neuroimaging_in_Anxiety_
Disorders

6. Wlassoff, V. (2015, January 24). How does post-
    traumatic stress disorder change the brain?
    [Blog post]. Retrieved from http://brainblogger.
    com/2015/01/24/how-does-post-traumatic-stress-
    disorder-change-the-brain/

7. Moore, M. S. (2011, July 6). PTSD brain studies look
    at hippocampus. *Pacific Standard*. Retrieved from
    https://psmag.com/news/ptsd-brain-studies-look-
    at-hippocampus-33419

8. Duke University Medical Center. (2012, November
    5). PTSD linked to smaller brain area regulating fear
    response. *Science Daily*. Retrieved from https://www.
    sciencedaily.com/releases/2012/11/121105161355.htm

9. The Anatomy of PTSD. (n.d.). Brainline. Retrieved
    from https://www.brainline.org/slideshow/
    anatomy-ptsd

10. Newton, P. (2009, January 29). The anatomy of
    posttraumatic stress disorder: What parts of the
    brain are involved in posttraumatic stress disorder?.
    Psychology Today. Retrieved from https://www.
    psychologytoday.com/blog/mouse-man/200901/the-
    anatomy-posttraumatic-stress-disorder

11. Brunette, L. (2003, February 6). Meditation
    produces positive changes in the brain. University
    of Wisconsin-Madison, Madison, WI. Retrieved
    from https://news.wisc.edu/meditation-produces-
    positive-changes-in-the-brain/

Chapter 9

1. Schering-Plough, Merck & Co. (2010, January 21). *New survey finds infertility delivers a serious blow to self-esteem* [Press release]. Retrieved from http://www.evaluategroup.com/Universal/View.aspx?type=Story&id=204824

Chapter 10

1. Grothaus, M. (2015, January 29). Why journaling is good for your health. (And 8 tips to get better). Retrieved from https://www.fastcompany.com/3041487/8-tips-to-more-effective-journaling-for-health

2. Adams, Kathleen. (2018). A short course in journal writing. It's easy to W.R.I.T.E. Retrieved from https://journaltherapy.com/lets-journal/a-short-course-in-journal-writing/

Chapter 12

1. Weir, K. (2012). The pain of social rejection. *American Psychological Association, 43*(4), 50. Retrieved from https://www.apa.org/monitor/2012/04/rejection.aspx

2. Azab, M. (2017, April 25). Is social pain real pain? Research shows that hurt feelings activate the same brain areas as physical pain. *Psychology Today*. Retrieved from https://www.psychologytoday.com/blog/neuroscience-in-everyday-life/201704/is-social-pain-real-pain

3. Walsh, B. (2015, March 23). The science of resilience: Why some children can thrive despite adversity. *Harvard Graduate School of Education: Usable Knowledge.* Retrieved from https://www.gse.harvard.edu/news/uk/15/03/science-resilience

4. Steuber, K. R., & High, A. (2015). Disclosure strategies, social support and quality of life in infertile women. *Human Reproduction, 30*(7), 1635-1642. doi:10.1093/humrep/dev093

Chapter 13

1. What is evidence-based practice (EBP)?. (n.d.). *Duke University Medical Center Library & Archives.* Retrieved from http://guides.mclibrary.duke.edu/c.php?g=158201&p=1036021

Chapter 14

1. Saakvitne, K. W., Pearlman, L. A., & The Staff of TSI/CAAP. (1996). *Transforming the pain: A workbook on vicarious traumatization* (pp. 63-66). New York, NY: W.W. Norton & Company, Inc.

Made in the USA
Monee, IL
28 April 2021

67137992R00079